HRD for
Developing States
and Companies

*Proceedings of the 2005
Brunei Darussalam AEMC Convention*

EDITED BY

ABDUL GHANI PG HJ METUSIN

OOI KEE BENG

ASEAN-EC MANAGEMENT CENTRE
Brunei Darussalam

INSTITUTE OF SOUTHEAST ASIAN STUDIES
Singapore

First published in Singapore in 2005 by
ISEAS Publications
Institute of Southeast Asian Studies
30 Heng Mui Keng Terrace
Pasir Panjang
Singapore 119614

E-mail: publish@iseas.edu.sg
Website: http://bookshop.iseas.edu.sg

The responsibility for facts and opinions in this publication rests exclusively with the authors and their interpretations do not necessarily reflect the views or the policy of the publisher or its supporters.

ISEAS Library Cataloguing-in-Publication Data

HRD for developing states and companies / edited by Abdul Ghani Pg. Hj. Metusin and Ooi Kee Beng.
  1.   Employees—Training of.
  2.   Personnel management.
  3.   Manpower planning.
  I.   Abdul Ghani Pg. Hj. Metusin.
  II. Ooi, Kee Beng, 1955–
HF5549.5 T7H912   2005

ISBN 981-230-332-4 (soft cover)
ISBN 981-230-333-2 (hard cover)

Typeset by Superskill Graphics Pte Ltd
Printed in Singapore by Photoplates Pte Ltd

Contents

Competence Development

Corporate Experiences

Foreword

The coming into being of this volume is a milestone in the achievements of the ASEAN-EC Management Centre (AEMC). It will extend the reach of the type of generative ideas that gave form to the many chapters in this book authored by both famous statesmen and successful business consultants. It is furthermore the crowning achievement of the institution's director, Abd Ghani Pg Hj Metusin, and his capable and loyal staff.

As with all valuable books, avid readers will find pearls of wisdom in this anthology that attempt to bridge the unnecessarily wide gap between state governance and business management. It contains much useful advice for the practical person as well as the theoretically minded.

Pg Dato Paduka Haji Abd Hamid bin Pg Hj Mohd Yassin
Permanent Secretary at the Prime Minister's Office
Brunei Darussalam

Preface

Brunei Darussalam has a small population and our people are our vital assets in nation building. We wish to develop a modern, diversified and sustainable economy. To achieve this successfully, we need to enhance our human capacity so as to give our families and communities lasting confidence in the future.

At the heart of this vision are our people.

His Majesty the Sultan of Brunei, in a statement made during the APEC High Level Forum on Human Capacity Building for Common Prosperity held in Beijing about four years ago, stressed that due to the rapid advancement of technology and communications, it was important to update constantly the skills of our people and such skills had to be brought to an international level of competitiveness. And for them to prosper in the New Economy, they had to feel that they had a personal stake in its success. The challenge here was obviously the complexity of the skills and knowledge to be absorbed and mastered by our people.

Since then, we have put more focus on developing human resources as a key investment in our economy. It has therefore been given the utmost priority in our National Development Plan.

Brunei Darussalam is currently undertaking a consultative study to review and improve on the present state of human resource development policies and programmes. It essentially takes into account the evaluation of educational, academic, vocational, technical and related programmes carried out in the country. What we are aiming at is a comprehensive formulation that best serves the need of human resource development in our country.

We recognize the new demands placed on both the government and the private sector by the sheer speed of modernization, and the human qualities it calls for. These challenges, brought among others by the new competitive reality and by rapid globalization, require new mindsets and competencies, and innovative ways of learning and training.

The chapters in this volume represent a giant stride in Brunei's efforts to strengthen the competitiveness of our people through continuous learning, unlearning and relearning. They were all originally papers presented at the convention — "HR Challenges & Opportunities in the New Economy" —

organized by the ASEAN-EC Management Centre, which was held on 18–20 January 2005 at Brunei's International Convention Centre.

We are living in a time when a new economic paradigm characterized by speed, innovation, short cycles, quality and productivity growth highlights intangible assets such as brand recognition, knowledge, innovation, and particularly, human capital. Essentially, it marks the beginning of a golden age for human resources, where human capital is regarded as the foundation of value creation.

People's talents, abilities, skills, adaptability to change, knowledge, attitudes, enthusiasm and the wisdom of leaders and managers to make the right decisions are the fundamentals for the success of any organization. Such qualities are required more than ever in today's world.

This convention clearly acknowledged this, as do governments and all successful businesses. They now recognize that human resource development has become a field of research, academic study and debate in its own right. It has moved beyond the purely administrative considerations it has traditionally offered and now enjoys a status that invites a broader, more pro-active and more strategic role in both government and business activities.

It is important for human resource practitioners to constantly widen and deepen their knowledge to enable them to deliver their thoughts and ideas with assurance and credibility. It is also important that their decisions stand the test of time for sustaining their countries' economic and social development.

There is a growing realization that they need to be able to work on problem-focused and solution-driven issues in multi-disciplinary teams that are capable of developing strategies that support and drive business growth. Inevitably, these expectations impose new demands on international executives and practitioners charged with developing and implementing those economic and business strategies. We must remain aware of the complexity of human resource development in the New Economy and the challenges it poses.

To be aware of a challenge is one thing. It is equally important for us to have an open mind when considering the ideas suggested by international studies and researchers.

This is where we need the help, advice and support of professional experts from all over the world, in constructing real solutions to human resource development issues and in assessing strengths and weaknesses, prioritizing areas of challenge and determining practical strategies.

HRH Paduka Seri Pengiran Anak Puteri Hajah Masna

Editorial Remarks

One of the main themes of the convention on which the chapters of this book are based was the connection between state governance and business management. To do justice to this gravely important relationship, we have therefore chosen to divide the volume basically into two sections. The first and shorter one deals mainly with human resource development (HRD) as a political undertaking. In essence, this amounts to a collection of advice for statesmen. The tone setter here is Tun Dr Mahathir Mohamad's presentation of how culture, skills, and development are interconnected, and how serious change must involve serious cultural innovations.

The second section — which deals with HRD as a central concern in national and international companies — is subdivided into three parts. The first part deals with various elements that make up strategic thought in HRD, the second concentrates on discussions and practical plans for the development of competence in corporations, while the third consists of descriptions of HRD experiences in the corporate world.

Some chapters are in effect rapporteur notes made during the convention, which have then been complemented with information from electronic slide presentations. It is hoped that we have managed to capture the general essence of all the talks given at the convention. All presentations, excepting one omitted in accordance with the speaker's employer policy, are included here to provide as comprehensive an idea as possible of the range of topics discussed at the convention.

The rapporteur team consisted of volunteers from the Faculty of Business, Economics and Policy Studies, University of Brunei Darussalam (UBD), the Institute of Southeast Asian Studies (ISEAS), Singapore, and Institut Teknologi Brunei (ITB):

Dr Ooi Kee Beng (Head Rapporteur, ISEAS)
Dr Noorashikin Abdul Rahman (ISEAS)
Mr S. Thyaga Rajan (ISEAS)
Ms Norainie Ahmad (UBD)
Mr Ak Hj Mohd Hasnol Alwee bin Pg Hj Md Salleh (UBD)

Mr Suhaimi Hj Ali (UBD)
Mr Fairul Rizal Hj Rashid (UBD)
Ms Sophiana Chua Abdullah (ITB)

Abdul Ghani Pg Hj Metusin & Ooi Kee Beng
The Editors

Acknowledgements

The organizers of the ASEAN-EC International HRD Convention & Exhibition held in Brunei Darussalam on 18–20 January 2005 wish to thank Her Royal Highness Princess Hajah Masna, the former Prime Minister of Malaysia Tun Dr Mahathir Mohamad, the Permanent Secretary at the Prime Minister's Office of Brunei Darussalam Pg Dato Paduka Haji Abd Hamid bin Pg Hj Mohd Yassin, all esteemed speakers at the convention, chairpersons, supporting agencies, committee members and individuals, voluntary helpers, the rapporteurs from Singapore's Institute of Southeast Asian Studies and the University of Brunei Darussalam, and all others involved in making the milestone convention a reality and for helping to spread the many vibrant ideas aired there through this printed volume.

Special thanks to our Platinum sponsors Brunei Shell Petroleum Co., Brunei BLNG, and Brunei Shell Marketing; our Gold sponsors Citineon Brunei, TED Sdn. Bhd., and The Centrepoint Hotel; our Silver sponsors BAG Network & Accenture, Digi-Page, Radio Television Brunei (as our official broadcaster) and Sin Hup Huat Co; our Bronze sponsors Mitsubishi Corporation, IBB, IDBB, BearingPoint, Asia Insurance, PSA Muara, Archipelago Group, Brunei Press, Royal Brunei Catering, Interhouse Co., Anthony Tours, Hotmart and Galfer; our supporting agencies ASEAN Secretariat (based in Jakarta), Asia-Europe Foundation (based in Singapore), Brunei Economic Development Board, Institute of Southeast Asian Studies (Singapore), Malaysian Institute of Management, and Singapore Human Resource Institute, and various other organizations and individuals who have given us their support and encouragement. We also acknowledge the efforts and cooperation of our co-partner, Specialist Management Resource of Malaysia and exhibition manager Transpower Group.

Introduction

Learning is an ongoing process, and in these times learning must involve networking beyond national boundaries. With that in mind, the ASEAN-EC Management Centre (AEMC) decided to optimize its contacts within the region's HR community in order to manage a convention that would leave deep and lasting impressions on all involved. This was how the initiative to organize the ASEAN-EC International HRD Convention & Exhibition held on 18–20 January 2005 came about.

There is much we can learn from one another. Being introduced to a variety of perspectives within a single context can often inspire. Our adopted views are then necessarily challenged and their limitations made obvious.

The three-day event was an instructive one where delegates learned from others as much as they taught them. The fact that Her Royal Highness Paduka Seri Pengiran Anak Puteri Hajah Masna consented to officiate at the convention and that Tun Dr Mahathir Mohamad, the former Prime Minister of Malaysia, agreed to deliver the main keynote address were ample proof of how vital the subject of human resource development (HRD) is now considered to be even by statesmen. The conditions for doing business can no longer be considered apart from the challenges of nation building.

A warm word of gratitude must go to the Permanent Secretary at the Prime Minister's Office Brunei Darussalam, Pg Dato Paduka Haji Abd Hamid bin Pg Hj Mohd Yassin, for his continued support and advice. Without his persistence, the convention would not have been possible.

Besides Tun Dr Mahathir, seven other speakers delivered keynote papers, including the Minister of Education of Brunei Darussalam, the Honourable Pehin Dato Haji Abdul Aziz, who spoke on the need for continuous learning in order to remain competitive in a world overwhelmed by technological advancement and change. The common message given by all other keynote speakers — Günther Stahl, David Scruggs, Roberto F. de Ocampo, Dr Palan, David Cory and Christopher Mills — was *the vital importance of HRD in the New Economy.*

The three-day convention was designed to encourage dynamic interaction and brainstorming through discussions and networking sessions. This gave practical meaning to what most delegates intended to realize from the gathering, namely learning to achieve organizational growth by developing skills for handling change and challenge.

We hope that this volume will provide guidelines for HRD practitioners throughout the world and exert a significant and positive impact on future trends of thought in the field. This book is a humble attempt to raise HRD to a new level. We are after all merely a part of a much larger process — a process of learning, growing and creating. These proceedings should be able to serve as a handy, quick and useful reference for reflections on some major issues in HR facing not only Brunei Darussalam, but also other countries in the world.

The publication of this book would not have been possible without the assistance of our team of rapporteurs recruited from among lecturers at the University of Brunei Darussalam and researchers from the Institute of Southeast Asia Studies (ISEAS) Singapore, headed by Dr Ooi Kee Beng (ISEAS).

What was special about the convention was that it attempted to set trends in the field of HRD, rather than follow trends. Some of the distinguished speakers at the convention are renowned for breaking new ground both in state governance and in business management and were carefully chosen by us for their proven expertise.

The three days of discussions were more than just another event in the world of conferencing. The convention must be understood as part of a much larger process of *learning, teaching, adaptation and innovation*. We must all remember one thing. After all the talks and discussions — and the reading — must come ACTION, if everything we have done is to mean anything.

Let me quote Ali Sidikin of Indonesia: *Manusia tanpa cita-cita adalah mati, cita-cita tanpa kerja hanyalah mimpi* (An individual without ambition lacks life, having ambition without acting on it is but daydreaming).

The issues raised at the convention and in this book must be allowed to grow within the listener and the reader. Change has been the most commonly used term throughout the convention. My humble understanding is that we must change ourselves before we can change others.

Abdul Ghani Pg Hj Metusin

HRD FOR STATESMEN

1

Human Resource Development in Developing Countries

Tun Dr Mahathir Mohamad

The story of human civilization is the story of human resource development. The societies that were able to develop and progress were the societies that succeeded in developing and harnessing human resources.

Those unable to develop human resources remained backward and oftentimes became dominated by those with developed human resources.

Initially the stress was on brawn, the brute strength that enables hard laborious work to be done. Intelligence was not at a premium. Moving huge boulders to build the pyramids in the end depended on large numbers of well-built workers. On their own, the workers would not have been able to accomplish what they did, but the supervisors and the engineers applied the brute strength of the workers to achieve the wonders that we still see today.

The societies that developed themselves based on human resources became stratified with manual workers at the bottom and the others above, graded according to their level of skill and intelligence. Those able to manage human resources would attain the highest level. In themselves, they constituted the highest level of human resource.

In many societies, the stratification became institutionalized and embedded in the culture. It became even a part of their beliefs and religions. This is what we have to this day.

In most societies, a very complex system of castes based on the specialization of labour and occupation tends to make an appearance. Once this happens, the upward mobility of the lower castes is hindered. Much potential is lost.

But in some societies, the stratification is not very rigid and it is possible for skills to be developed by the lower caste to the extent that upward mobility is attained. The more upwardly mobile the human resources, the greater will the availability of developed human resources be.

Today, outwardly at least, we do not believe in castes or stratification. Members of any stratum can move up or down as they are able, and society benefits because the potential of all can be exploited to the maximum.

It is this realization that has made human resource development an important matter for any society wishing to progress.

If we look back again at history we will see cases of backward nations developing into very sophisticated and powerful civilizations. On the other hand, we will also see some highly developed nations regressing, and we will find that the progression is really the result of the developing or the deteriorating of human resources.

We all know how Peter the Great of Russia changed his very backward nation into one of the most powerful in the world. He forced his people to acquire the skills of Western Europe until they were able to excel in the particular skills that he, Peter, considered necessary for the ambitions he had for Mother Russia. It was human resource development on a massive national scale, achieved through the autocratic power that Peter and his successors wielded.

The modernization of Russia is something that people interested in human resource development should study. Since the Russian tsars were primarily interested in making Russia a great power and expanding its territories, they trained their people in the design, production and application of weapons of war.

To this day, Russians are unable to produce quality consumer goods, but are able to invent, design and build the most effective war machines. These may not be as sophisticated as the war machines of the West, but they serve the Russians well enough.

This ability is the result of selective human resource development. No doubt if the Russians really want to, they can produce the best radios or televisions or motorcars, and other consumer goods, but their priority has always been guns, tanks, aeroplanes, rockets and nuclear bombs. And not even the Americans are prepared to test these weapons by going to war with them. Russian human resource development has achieved the target the Russians had aimed for.

This raises questions about why the Russians can produce first-class weapons but not first-class shoehorns. It is all about the focus in human resource development.

Actually, skills can be acquired and honed to a high degree purely through focus and effort. The Orang Asli of Malaysia may not be good academically but they are good woodcarvers. Similarly, we know that the Balinese are good woodcarvers though they may lack other skills.

They are all very ordinary people but because their focus, concentration, and effort are on woodcarving, they acquire these skills, simply because that is what they want to do, or what their religion urges them to do. They begin very young, probably whittling away at pieces of wood as soon as they can handle a knife. Over time not only will their fingers and hands coordinate well for the purpose of carving, their whole body develops and adapts to positions best suited for woodcarving. As they do this over and over again, the quality of their work improves. Their dexterity and speed also improve constantly.

Invariably, some will be better than others. But all will be better woodcarvers than people who are not from a community of woodcarvers.

This begs another question. Why are people from a community skilled in a particular craft much more likely to become skilful in that craft than people from outside the community? It would seem, and this is my personal and unscientific opinion, that skills are inherited. The children of craftsmen are more able to master their father's craft than children of people not skilled in the craft concerned.

Now if this is true, the acquisition of skills by the parents will in fact be passed on to the children, and each generation will inherit the skill of the previous generation. If we care to be observant, we will notice that this is happening all the time.

We know that the human race acquires more and more skills with each generation. Our generation today is more skilful in whatever we do than our fathers' generation and our fathers' generation was more skilful than our grandfathers' generation. Certainly we are more skilful and more able in whatever we do than our ancestors of long ago.

Is our high skill simply due to our conscious effort to acquire the skills of the past generation or is it because we inherited these skills and were able to get a head start, so to speak? We do not have to invent the wheel because not only has it been invented, but improvements have also been made to it, and if we care to do so we can improve on the improvement. Without thinking of the original crude wheel, we can start from the latest sophisticated wheel, such as those used in aircraft landing gears for example, and improve on it. All the accumulated knowledge of the past seems to be ours without us having to go through the long process of development that the wheel had gone through.

If we inherit the skills of our forebears, then our own skills, honed in our lifetime, will also be inherited by our children. If that is so then the benefit and the returns on human resource development are far more than that which accrues to our generation. We are actually contributing to the development of future generations.

If we develop a whole community, then that community will become more and more skilled with the passage of time. Moreover, the skills and the values that accompany them will become a part of the culture of the community.

The Balinese people are, again, a prime example. For them, woodcarving and stylised painting are a part of the culture of the community. In fact, these are directly linked to the religion they profess. And that culture will be inherited by future generations. Once a skill becomes a part of the culture, then human resource in terms of the particular skill will just continue through the generations, improving with each generation.

In Malaysia, we have a problem. We have three different communities, each with different skills. Unfortunately, the skills of the indigenous community are not only less lucrative, but because they do not provide the community with a good living, the skills are dying out instead of improving. Besides, the skills were from an age when products wrought by hands were the only ones available. Today, practically all products are manufactured by others using modern techniques and machines. The hand-worked products of the indigenous people are no longer needed and they cannot retain and hone their skills simply because they do not have a need to. If they wish to survive and prosper then they need to learn new skills. Since they have not inherited these skills, they need time to acquire them. They may need several generations before the new skills become part of their culture. As the Russians have demonstrated, through persistence and focus, they can become as skilled as or even more skilled than the communities that already possess these skills.

As has been pointed out, a people not familiar with a particular skill will find it more difficult to master it in comparison with people who are already familiar. Doing business is part of the culture of the Chinese. They are familiar and skilful at it. The Malays have become monetized only recently and their business skills are much poorer than those of the Chinese.

What the Malays and other indigenous peoples in Malaysia need is business training as a part of Malaysia's human resource development. There is evidence that they are already acquiring some business skills, but their business acumen on the average is still inferior to that of the Chinese and Indians. Training will enable them to overcome the gap between them and the Chinese. Living in a Chinese business environment will also help.

If my theory is right that skills can be inherited and become a part of the culture, then the efforts at Malay human resource development in Malaysia will in time result in the handicap now faced by the Malays becoming less and less. Human resource development, provided it is carefully planned and assiduously carried out will not only develop and enhance the skills of the target group or the community, but will have long-term effects over generations.

A matter that needs serious attention in human resource development is employee attitude and work ethics. Far too often the stress is on skills, while attitude and ethics are given less attention.

Of the Asian peoples, the Japanese have shown the fastest capacity to acquire skills that were foreign to them. They not only made special efforts to acquire these skills but have a culture that enabled them to do so quickly and even better than their models.

The Japanese are very diligent and very meticulous. Their traditional handicrafts are of the highest quality. A sense of shame influences their attitude to work and the products they produce. Not producing the best would be shameful, and shame is enough for the Japanese to go to the length of committing suicide.

That sense of shame at work, of not being up to expectation, drives the Japanese to learn and to acquire exceptional skills. True, initially the Japanese produced goods of inferior quality, but there were instances even in the early period that the products of the Japanese could be far superior to the products of the people they were learning from.

Toyota started as a producer of textile weaving machines. The original machine was from Europe, but Toyota's machine was so superior that they were bought by the very people whose machine inspired the Toyota machine, and today no one questions the quality of Japanese products.

The success of the Japanese is partly due to the development of their human resources within the new industrial environment and within a culture that values diligence and attention to quality.

There are of course a whole lot of qualities that will enhance human resource development. Diligence and pride over the quality of the products are among the most important. Therefore when human resources are being developed, attention must be given to the development of the right attitudes and values. In fact, the development of these values is a crucial part of human resource development.

If human resource development is properly carried out, then whole new skills can be acquired and the value system or the culture of the people changed. The emergence of great new civilizations in human history is due to the development of human resources. The backward people and nations can become successful and great if human resource development is carried out properly, with proper balance between skills acquisition and the cultivation of good ethical values. It may take several generations but it can be done.

Human resource development gives hope to the poor and the backward peoples and nations that they too can develop and grow and possibly even catch up with others who are ahead. But in the first place, those in authority, the government in particular, must want to develop the people and the nation.

In the old days when governments were autocratic, it was possible for the government to force the development of human resources. This was what happened when Peter the Great of Russia decided to modernize his country and catch up with the Western European nations. But it may well happen that an autocratic ruler has no desire to develop his nation, in which case the autocracy spells doom for the nation.

Today, autocracy is frowned upon and only democracy is allowed, but a democratic government can be so engrossed with the politics of survival that it may not be able to focus on human resource development. The opposition in a democratic system can be so negative that nothing can be done without it trying to block the proposed action, and this includes human resource development. If we compare the progress of India and China, we will appreciate the effect of government systems and culture on human resource development. One is democratic and the other autocratic. When autocrats decide to develop, the speed can be formidable.

In a democracy, both the government and the opposition may really desire to develop the nation and its people may want to implement human resource development programmes. But the prolonged debates and the sniping at all government efforts can undermine the development and upgrading of human resources. Human resource development will take place but the process will take time.

Human resource development is therefore not just a case of making training available to target groups. It requires firstly vision and will from the government. That vision must be made the vision of the people as a whole.

To achieve this, the government of a democratic country needs to be strong enough to deflect the negativism of the opposition. In an autocratic country, the desire of those in authority to develop human resources is all-important.

If the vision is accepted by the people, then prior to or together with the skills training, there must be inculcated in the trainees the right set of values. They must appreciate that the training is good for them and good for their country. They must understand and appreciate the values that can contribute to the success of their development.

The trainees must also understand how, through repetition, they can acquire the necessary skills. More than that, the skills they acquire will probably be inherited by their children and their children's children.

In Malaysia, where the business and management skill level of the Malays and other indigenous people is far below that of the Chinese in particular, deliberate training and inculcation of good ethics and values can help them overcome the gap between the two races. Eventually, maybe after two or three generations, the skills and the ethics of the Malays and other indigenous people will match those of the people of the developed nations. When that happens then the inequalities in the development and well-being of the peoples of Malaysia will largely have disappeared.

Human resources development is therefore the factor that will determine the catching-up process and the progress of the developing nation. Of course, developed nations also need to develop their human resources, but their need to do this is less crucial than that of a developing nation.

There are really no intrinsic obstacles to the development of human resource. Obviously for those who are far behind in terms of human skills, a much longer period will be necessary. But with dedication and persistence, coupled with the willingness to repeat doing anything and everything no matter how difficult, over and over again, skills will be honed, and the ability, whether manual or intellectual, will be acquired. Progress will be geometrical rather than lineal. The skills will be inherited and become a part of the culture of the people, so that less deliberate pressure will be needed in the future.

Truly, the hope of the less developed peoples lies in human resource development. Assiduously implemented, the disparities within the community and between the nations will be reduced. It is difficult, it is frustrating, but we have no choice if we do not want to be forever dominated by those who, with a centuries-long head start, are far ahead.

2

Building the New HR Base — The Brunei Perspective

Pehin Dato Haji Awang Abdul Aziz Umar

We are faced with unprecedented change in our lifetime. It is not so much that there have been many changes, but rather it is the rate of change imposed upon most societies that has dramatically altered our socio-economic landscape. Increasingly rapid technological changes have affected the way we live, the way we work and how we conduct ourselves towards each other. Inevitably, these changes have an important bearing on the way nations and organizations develop their human resources.

Although change is inevitable, it is not necessarily a bad thing. What is important to address is how we *confront* change and the challenges that come with it. If we survey the way technology has affected socio-economic patterns, we find that before the twentieth century, "change" was relatively slow in comparison to a person's life expectancy. The time gap between the discovery of new technology and its mass application was very wide. That gap has gradually shrunk and the impact of change is being felt sooner than ever before. For instance, photography was invented in 1727, but it took 112 years before it was put to use. The telephone was invented in 1820 and it took 56 years before its application became general; television was invented in 1922 and was introduced to the general public 12 years later; the atomic bomb took only 6 years between its invention and its application in 1945; and the solar battery took only 2 years between its invention and its application in 1953.

In light of the rapid introduction of new technologies, the need for a person to keep abreast of new knowledge and skills means that periodic upgrading and retraining have become a necessity. More and more people are realizing that one-time education can no longer be regarded as an option if they wish to survive in an ever-changing world. Once upon a time, a person could adapt to a set of conditions that would remain more or less constant throughout his/her lifetime. One could simply gain a university degree and reasonably expect it to be economically relevant throughout one's career. With the rapidity of technological innovations, however, knowledge or skills gained in school quickly become obsolete. An electronic engineer, for instance, was at one time estimated to have between 10 to 15 years before his knowledge became obsolete. Today, it is estimated to be only around 2 years.

What has emerged in response to this new skills demand is a cycle of adaptation repeated several times within a single lifetime. A person leaving school today may need to be retrained at least five times in his working life. In the manufacturing industry, for instance, there is a demand for greater automation. Machines and robots, more efficient and better suited for mass production, may eventually replace manual jobs, which in turn will create a greater demand for a more skilled labour force. What becomes very clear to us is that gaining and/or maintaining competitiveness and meeting these increases in skilled labour demands is to be considered a strategic priority.

Changes in the world economy have laid increased emphasis on a labour force with specialized training skills. Occupation specialization has become necessary not only in acquiring a job, but also to simply hold on to it. The undereducated and unskilled person is more likely to be unemployed, remain unemployed or unemployable in many kinds of jobs. Yet, the supply of a labour force armed with economically relevant knowledge continues to lag behind contemporary demand.

Even those in the education and training sector are subject to these forces of change. When we consider the increasingly rapid pace of technological application, the question that almost naturally comes to mind is whether the educational sector is keeping pace with these advances. The knowledge and skills that teachers and trainers impart have to be current and constantly updated. The phenomenal rate at which knowledge is expanding does not make their task any easier. The amount of printed materials produced increases at approximately 8 to 10% annually; roughly half a million new books, 250,000 periodicals and journals, and 200,000 specialized reports appear on an increasingly diverse field. A child born today will live in a world with 32 times the amount of information by the time he reaches the age of 50. The individual will not be able to assimilate all the available information in one lifetime. A specialist in the field of medicine will have to devote every hour of his working life to reading everything published just to keep abreast of developments.

When we consider formal education as a process of systematic learning, confined to a narrow span of our lives, and that education in its current form can only provide all school-aged children with basic education, it is clear that it can never be enough to meet the growing skill demands required for work. A majority of these students go on to secondary education, an elite minority goes so far as to enrol for higher education courses and an even smaller number such as researchers go on to pursue lifelong education. Most leave school because they are unable to proceed further, most probably having failed in an examination system where only 40% of any cohort continue on to further or higher education. Once out of the school system, this group can expect to spend a lifetime at work, that is, if they are able to find employment. However, most of those who do will lack vocational education and training as a foundation for working life. A few are lucky enough to receive apprenticeships before joining the workforce but may never have the opportunity to undergo further training during their working lives.

In light of all this, what is the cost of meeting these growing demands? If we take a worker's average retirement age today to be 60, the amount of time that person spends learning and relearning new skills will never be able to economically justify the years he will work. Fifteen years of basic education — up to degree level — will have already consumed at least 21 years of a person's life, leaving less than 40 years for that person to utilize the skills he/she has acquired: a ratio of 1 year for every two he/she will work. If we add the further training that a person will need throughout their career, the training to work ratio will be even less. As a consequence, the relative price of educational services tends to rise. Public, enterprise and family budgets are under pressure to meet increases in the scope, quality and duration of education. Under these circumstances, what then is the economic value attached to those who are less fortunate or less talented or those who never had the opportunity to acquire basic education? They will fall far behind, with little or no hope of improving their circumstances. Their entire working lives will only be dedicated to serving the economic elite.

Brunei Darussalam embarked on a bilingual system of education soon after we achieved full sovereignty. Malay and English became the dominant languages of instruction. This has widened the opportunities available to our citizens for higher education in the English-speaking and Malay-speaking worlds. English language mastery for our youth is key to accessing institutions in the English-speaking world. In fact, some of our students do learn other languages in school, particularly Arabic, and have gone on to study in the Middle East or other parts of the world. With the increasing use of information communication technology (ICT) and the Internet, those who are competent in the English language are at an advantage in accessing knowledge through this technology, since most materials are written in the English language, both in hard copy and on the Internet.

Human resource development is not new to this country. Brunei Darussalam embarked on its plan as far back as the 1950s. It began sending many of its young citizens to study abroad, particularly in Malaysia, Singapore, the United Kingdom, Egypt and Australia. Most of our ministers, including myself, and senior government officers are products of the plan. Some have retired from public service though many have remained active in the private sector and are contributing to community development. The plan has continued to this present day and has been expanded to include sending students to other countries, such as Japan, Germany, the United States, Canada and New Zealand. However, more and more Bruneians are now educated locally from primary to tertiary levels, as we continue to develop our institutional capacity.

In developing our education system, Brunei Darussalam has seen major gains in the average educational attainment of its workforce, as older workers with lower educational attainment have retired and have been replaced by higher-educated, younger cohorts. While overall population growth will increasingly depend on longer life expectancy and new birth in the future, Bruneian "school-leavers" (those who complete their schooling in Brunei) will continue for the foreseeable future to remain the main source of new workers. However, current trends show a falling birth rate in this country. It was estimated at 2% in 2003. This downward trend continues despite the absence of governmental funds for family planning. This may change the demography towards an ageing population over the next 20 years. With a lower birth rate and more people living longer, people can remain active in the workforce well beyond the mandatory retirement age of 55. The good news is, as Brunei continues to develop its post-secondary education and provide more scholarships for its citizens, we can see rising levels of participation in post-secondary education. This will however not generate the same strong gains in labour force educational attainment that were seen in the past. Brunei's population increases, the growing sophistication of the economy and the need for greater numbers to be retrained place greater demand on our limited financial resources. Thus, further gains in overall human capital quality will increasingly have to come via lifelong learning beyond the formal schooling of youth.

In such a labour market, a key challenge is ensuring that those who enter the labour market have, through lifelong learning, the skills to meet employer needs. This requires a mix of skills, both higher and lower ones obtained through a continuum of educational attainment encompassing secondary school, technical/vocational college, trades apprenticeships, and university and post-graduate degrees. Brunei Darussalam will continue to place strong emphasis on developing its education programme at post-secondary levels. Skills will also have to match the specific kinds of jobs that are appearing. For example, biochemist jobs require biochemists, and not just chemists or other specialists.

In the area of learning, Brunei's government is committed, among other things, to improving the quality of education. This includes the provision of a good learning environment and highly trained teachers and effective school leaders. Institutional capacity enhancement, including the building of more vocational and technical schools, is also needed as is cooperation with the private sector to update labour market information to better reflect the realities of work in the twenty-first century, including the growth in self-employment, entrepreneurship and skills upgrading.

For Brunei's Ministry of Education to develop effectively as an organization that is capable of supporting the human resource development plan of the country, it too has to have a sound governance framework, including developing a long-term, say a 20-year, strategic plan with sustainable outcomes, and hopefully a detailed activities programme at the departmental level.

What I feel is important to highlight here is the need for society to recognize the vicious cycle that we ourselves have created; that society does not compose entirely of people who are very talented or fortunate; that technological advancements cannot be expressed purely on economic terms; and that a person's productivity cannot be measured only by his/her ability to create greater profit for the few. The fact remains that even if we can produce a better-educated and better-skilled workforce, the very purpose of modern technology to reduce dependency on expensive human labour means that only a small minority will eventually profit from these advances. The basic economic law of supply and demand will dictate that even if every single person entering the job market holds a university degree, only a few can be absorbed, thus mitigating the value of such a qualification.

Having said this, while greater efforts to introduce better-educated and highly skilled workers into the market cannot be neglected, the fortunate must not ignore the plight of those who have fallen in this pursuit. The disasters of the past few weeks (such as the tsunamis), although tragic, have provided opportunity for an unprecedented level of international cooperation and support for the affected peoples. The plight of the hundreds of thousands of mostly poor people has touched the conscience of the global community. Clothes, food, medicine and money have poured in from all over the world. I am truly touched by the spirit of volunteerism and altruism shown towards victims of the disaster. It is times like these that make us human. Generosity and compassion manage to overcome our mortal deficiencies — greed and apathy.

What these past events have demonstrated is that despite the economic and financial pressures of daily life, pressures to produce grander profit — goodness and compassion — are alive and well. When we develop and train our human resources, it should not be simply about producing better-skilled workers but positive members of society as well. The need is to mould and train highly skilled workers while imbuing them with the moral and ethical insight that they can positively contribute towards society as a whole. While preparing our youth for their future careers, emphasis must also be placed upon their moral and ethical makeup. Basic values such as honesty, integrity and compassion have long been taken for granted. The rise in white-collar crimes in the world is indicative of a growing decadence among the political and corporate elite. One often reads of corruption, fraud and the abuse of power, so synonymous with the so-called "talented few", which have become an almost daily occurrence. One may need to be reminded: intelligence, skill and talent are like knives — they cut both ways.

For these reasons, we in Brunei Darussalam seek to integrate fully a system for preparing our youth with the skills and tools required for workers of the future. Lifelong learning habits need to be embraced by individuals so that the community becomes a learning society. Every child must be taught to be a self-directed and independent learner so that when they enter the working world, they too will become lifelong learners. At the same time, they are instilled with Islamic learning and values that espouse honesty, truthfulness, integrity, accountability and compassion. Our integrated curriculum, commonly referred to here as "*kurikulum bersepadu*", is designed to bring elements of these values into the regular school curriculum alongside other school subjects, rather than having these taught separately in religious schools and national schools. The education of our future generation should be holistic, and should consider spiritual, mental and physical development as a whole rather than separate segments. Hopefully, this will help shape our children as responsible individuals and citizens. We also hope they will grow up as happy children and enter adulthood with fond memories of their school years and establish bonds that last a lifetime.

Islam is often misunderstood by non-Muslims but also by some of its followers. Some may say that religion, particularly Islam, has no place in the modern world. Is it because many of us have a poor or fragmented understanding of our own religious identity and this in turn brings about a vast chasm of conflicting beliefs that are difficult to reconcile? Can it also be that different groups of the Ummah adhere to only a few of its fundamental principles, particularly those that fit their own agenda, that Islam becomes easily hijacked by a zealous minority? I do not have a ready answer for this. However, there is a need for us to examine the reason why the inability to work together as a coherent Ummah leads others to view Islam as a modern problem. Although many Muslims feel that there is an unfair characterization of Islam throughout the world, the reality is that we Muslims have yet to identify the common factors among ourselves and to lead our lives in a manner that is compatible with the teachings of this faith of peace. At one point in time, the Islamic civilization led the world in science, medicine, mathematics and engineering. Baghdad was once the seat of higher learning, not the centre of so much strife and despair.

Our goal is to create societies that are not only in tune with changes brought about by modern technologies, but more importantly to ensure that we have societies that are responsible, honest and compassionate. True economic growth cannot be achieved without workers at all levels, from the very top to the lowest rungs of the organizational ladder, performing in a manner that can induce greater productivity. At the same time, we must not allow what we have already achieved to be destroyed by an irresponsible few. Giant multinational companies have collapsed when a few people overcome by greed decide to use their so-called "talent" to enrich themselves unfairly. Some nations blessed with abundant natural and human resources have disintegrated because their social fabric has been ripped apart by rampant dishonest practices. No amount of technological training and re-training can repair the harm caused by such talented but corrupt individuals. At the same time, we must not ignore the fact that these individuals are also products of our own society. It is society that shapes the values an individual espouses. For any nation, the consequences of irresponsible behaviour can be quite devastating. For these reasons, religious, moral and ethical values must go hand-in-hand with skills development.

We have tried to learn from the lessons of other nations, the numerous success stories as well as the failures, in the hope that we too can achieve the same successes and avoid the same mistakes. More importantly, we try to learn the lessons of our own history so that we can achieve greater things and be aware of our past errors. In our schools, children are told of the events of our past so that they can understand the present, and hopefully can dream of the future. Our people are our greatest assets. However, no matter what skills they attain or how much talent they possess; those skills and talents must contribute towards the common good. Arrogance, greed and apathy have been the cause of so much suffering. As the saying goes: "History tends to repeats itself". Is it because man never learns?

3

Managing and Achieving Excellence through HR Key Performance

K.Y. Mustapha

ABOUT SABAH

It is a huge state, the second largest in Malaysia, 73,000 sq. km in area, with a population of 2.6 million. It is highly agricultural, with a strong reliance on the tourism industry. It is similar to Sarawak and Brunei in that the manufacturing industry is very small.

In 1995, the 15-year Outline Perspective Plan was launched, and will end in 2010.

In 2003, the plan was revised and called the Halatuju Plan (Strategic Direction), with three areas of focus, namely, agriculture, tourism and manufacturing. The new emerging areas that Malaysia intends to focus on are biotechnology — which everybody talks about and which Malaysia is strong in — information and telecommunication.

CHALLENGES

The convergences of IT or ICT (Information Communication Technology) has led to many challenges, and Malaysia, being an open economy, has been forced to face them.

This means that a state like Sabah can no longer survive on its old economic system. To a nation or a state, a borderless world carries a lot of consequences. Globalization counts for a lot, and cultural, political, religious, and biological diversity must also be taken into account.

Malaysia, however, feels it can handle these challenges. Sabah itself is very diverse. Cultural diversity is no longer the problem now that it was in the early days. The idea of Bangsa Malaysia does not mean that everyone must be turned into Malays. Instead, all ethnic races can retain cultural, religious and ethnic identity, and live together in harmony. Misunderstandings on this point have been utilized politically in some quarters.

Sabah has seen a change of government every decade or so, and a stronger mandate was gained in the last elections, which did not involve any change in government. However, something important did occur, which harks back to the issue of handling cultural diversity and the economy. A stronger mandate was given to the government. Sabah has shown itself to be a politically experienced state. No particular religious group dictates religious matters in Sabah. Muslims are slightly more in number but this majority is not as clear as it is in other states. In other states, Muslims are Malays, but in Sabah, the Muslim community include Bajau, Dusun, Murus, Brunei and Kadazan. For example, in Ranau in the centre of Sabah, there is a large Muslim community that by racial background are Dusuns. Due to the nature of Sabah, there can be no dominant ethnic group.

BIOLOGICAL DIVERSITY

There has been a lot of emphasis recently on the biological diversity of Sabah. In the past, Sabah relied totally on timber, which is its main natural resource and much of the timber resources were cut down. Suffice it to say that this was due to the need to fulfil the goals of development, which included large investments in the building of the infrastructure. Timber was required to finance this aim.

Lately, Sabah's economic base has diversified. No longer is it purely reliant on timber. It has now also moved into agriculture and tourism. There are over one million hectares of land planted with oil palm and other resources. There is a focus on protecting bio-diversity.

Another challenge is resource distribution among the people of Sabah, and the divide between rich and poor, rural and urban, and the digitally knowledgeable and the digitally illiterate. A few years ago, there was much discussion about the k-economy and the federal government sought the opinion of the Sabah government. Today, this is one area Sabah wants to focus on. Half the population of Sabah lives in the rural areas and thus enjoy lower standards of living than people in the state or national capitals. Developing the rural sectors and transforming the economy has become a top priority.

The digital divide was discussed in the k-economy master plan and this has now been completed. It takes into account what the actual problems in Malaysia are, and is not based on central planning or on what the federal government thinks it knows, but on what people on the ground feel about the issue. The views are solicited by the government itself.

With regard to the language divide, 10 to 15 years ago, the English language issue was sensitive due to party politics. There were parties that were strong supporters of Bahasa Malaysia. However, now the reality of English as the key to knowledge has taken root. Malaysia is a pragmatic country and has to anticipate and understand the needs of the global economy and the pressure from international economic forces. English is the language of the Internet and the language of knowledge today. However, due to the system of education that emphasized Bahasa Malaysia, switching to English has become a major challenge. As said by Dr Mahathir, Malaysia has to be firm on this matter and continue to seek a higher standard in English. It is not possible to translate all the knowledge currently available in English into Bahasa Malaysia. A knowledge divide is therefore also a problem.

Developing countries, due to their nationalism and their newly independent status, tend to focus on language and culture, but realize a little late that they have been overtaken by major, mainly economic, events.

There are scattered islands of knowledge in Sabah, possessed only by some individuals. As in the past, knowledge is not readily shared and it has not been as easy as previously thought. Sharing knowledge is a major challenge. It is not done readily enough. The paradox is that "the more we share, the more powerful we become".

However, there is now a clearly articulated policy statement, which is the vision: "Transform Sabah into a prosperous, knowledgeable and civil society".

The mission statement outlines what is required: "A reinvented State Government that transforms Sabah into a knowledge-based society, with the following qualities/values:

- A Result-oriented, Responsible and Respected State Government Administration;
- A knowledgeable, effective and trustworthy State Public Service;
- A pleasant and open work environment that promotes transparency and a continuous learning culture; and
- A fully networked and functioning Electronic Government System."

There is now a need for the transformation of the public service sector in Sabah, specifically to improve inter-government operations. Today, there are ever-increasing demands on the public service sector, amid depleting resources, declining revenue and increasing complexity in the tasks required.

The future can be brighter if the public service sector transforms itself into a customer-centric, result-driven organization that emphasizes One Government. The key elements of change should not only take into account systems and processes, but also the fact the people can be complex and thus difficult to change. Thus, change should be sought in mindset, attitudes, perceptions, leadership, knowledge/skills and the sharing of knowledge sets.

PAST AND CURRENT EFFORTS

The work ethics of the Japanese and Koreans focused on by the "Look East" Policy are considered suitable to Malaysian culture and have thus been adopted as a development model by us. Currently, our efforts handle models such as "Malaysia Incorporated" and privatization partnerships between the government and private sector.

Also, the Circular on Administrative Reforms in the Civil Service of Malaysia has outlined the ideas behind the private and public partnership that Malaysia is currently adopting. Since the early 1990s, this has aimed at enhancing effectiveness and efficiency in the public service sector. Some examples include the MS-ISO, QCC, counter-service, TQM, client charter, benchmarking, etc.

The push for e-government (1997) has been a cornerstone of the effort by the state to improve public service in Sabah. Also, the state has stressed the importance of Public Service Integrity (Arahan Perdana Menteri 1/98) with a commitment to excellent service principles in public service. Needless to say, empowerment may be very important but at the same time, we cannot do without trust and trustworthiness.

The state has also focused on adapting to the changing needs of the external environment, as shown in its efforts at "Reinventing Government" in 1999. This has also been accompanied by what has been termed K-Public Service, or knowledge public service.

There has also been a commitment to rejuvenation, as exemplified by the "Succession Planning and Management Programme" of 2002. In addition, training is also important, as knowledge gaps need to be reduced in preparation for the future. A key feature of this is known as Residual Training Projects, which share knowledge and experiences among junior staff and pass on key aspects of public service practices.

LOOKING TO THE FUTURE

Sabah has always recognized its people as its main and most important resource. For the future, its main tasks will be strengthening e-government, reinventing government (RG) and the ongoing development of leadership.

The importance of e-government is that it brings the government closer to the citizens and delivers service "anytime, anywhere, anyhow". Sabah also hopes to institutionalize RG implementation for the future.

Also, Sabah is keen to strengthen service delivery mechanisms and shift from being service provider to being service enabler or manager. In increasing the usage of technology in the public service sector, Sabah intends to foster cooperation and collaboration through electronic means, thus building and sharing data and information.

As mentioned earlier, the focus will be on the people — our most valuable asset. In this regard, the emphasis will be on "Lifelong Learning" and the "Learning Organization". The public service will also emphasize "service beyond self" and foster a culture of lifelong dedication and excellence within the public service sector.

The intention is to eventually develop private sector/community governance such as Malaysia Inc. The definition of good government is "A Public Service that provides the best services and information, understands and provides services actually needed by the people. It also ensures that services and advices are fully felt and enjoyed by the people, especially the rural community".

Good governance is reflected in the manner in which power is exercised in the management of a country's (or state's) social and economic resources.

Good governance also means strengthening the four pillars of governance, namely, accountability, transparency, predictability and participation. In this, tools such as the Corruption Perceptions Index will be useful in assessing these pillars and in finding ways to strengthen them.

In conclusion, the question that needs to be asked is who is doing the measuring when we talk about performance measurement. For the public sector, good performance indicators would include economic performance, social development, standard of living, socio-political stability, the level of corruption and the number of public complaints. However, no single measurement is sufficient and any system needs continuous improvement. It must be said that one should never compromise on diligence, quality, passion, ethics and integrity.

4

Achieving an Integrated, Informed and Innovative Government for the Twenty-first Century — A Model for Emerging Markets

Ayman Adhair

A methodology for achieving an integrated, informed and innovative government for the twenty-first century can build on three concepts:

- International Best Practice — Embracing international benchmarks.
- Modern Public Management Theory — Utilizing relevant concepts.
- Country-Specific Orientation, Values and Commitment.

Some common issues faced by governments of emerging economies including Brunei Darussalam are:

- The role of the ministry is often not clearly stated and its organizational structure is often out of date and reflects old concepts.
- Management methods are often old style and not relevant to a modern environment.
- Service delivery is generally poor.
- The tasks and the person hired are often mismatched in terms of quality and quantity.
- Performance measurement is not practised efficiently.
- The development of information technology is often unplanned, fragmented and significantly under-utilized.

A point worth discussing here is the professionalism of the public service. The public service is a corporation formed by all government employees, and is not an entity or institution. It is therefore necessary that government employees believe that they work for the government and not for individual ministries. The employees must be embedded with a strong corporate culture based on sound management practice, delegation of power and accountability. They must also comply to a uniform code of ethics.

An organization must possess effective policy-making elements in terms of transparent vision, mission and strategies or policies. An organization must have key processes and tools including standardized HRM, IT, corporate planning and service delivery. It must also possess human resources that are capable and motivated enough to carry out their duties using the key processes and tools implemented by the agencies for achieving the desire goals. At the same time, the employees must also be provided with clear job specifications and training so that they can utilize their potential and do their job. The government's functions can be divided into two parts:

1. Agreed-upon core government function that can be divided into new functions to be developed and functions to be re-specified.
2. Existing government functions can be divided into two as well, i.e., functions that are to be re-specified (just like above) and functions that the government will no longer undertake.

Where agreed-upon core government functions are concerned, new functions that are to be developed and functions that are to be re-specified can be directly carried out by the ministry and/or some functions can be assigned to non-ministry structures that are accountable to the minister.

Certain functions that the government will no longer be responsible for can be undertaken by the private sector, with the government still maintaining a regulatory role, in some cases, for a transitional period.

As far as human resource development is concerned, all the attributes below must be carried out in an effective manner. These are work processes, management process, leadership, organization and job design, reward/recognition, organization and individual competency and behaviour and culture.

The government's vision is of vital importance. Information technology should be used as a strategic driver and enabler to create an integrated, innovative and informed government, aligned with the overall government direction. All organizational processes must be highly integrated and supported by the strategic use of modern, integrated information technology.

Incremental approaches in emerging economies will not work. Instead, a wide-ranging and fundamental approach is required. This should cover all levels of the government's hierarchy. In addition, the government requires careful design, sequencing and management of implementation. This might be a lot of work, but the results will be worth the effort. These will include an effective government, modern professional public service, vibrant private sector and strong well-served communities.

5

Human Resource Development — Challenges for the Public Services

Zainal Abiddin Tinggal

THE PUBLIC SERVICE CONUNDRUM: CHANGES IN THE PUBLIC SERVICE

Traditionally the public service sector was characterized by a stronger emphasis on processes and inputs than on results. This of course involved what was normally considered a distinctive "public service" approach to organization, service delivery and security of employment. Furthermore, where policy advice to governments was concerned, a sort of monopoly existed, where an entrenched system of preference conserved central control over personnel practices and conditions.

However, the major characteristics of the public service today include flexibility regarding processes, accountability for outputs and outcomes, and a strong emphasis on efficiency. There are now also strong similarities with the private sector in terms of organization and service delivery. Besides, the private sector is being used more and more for the delivery of public services.

The responsibility for policy advice is also being shared with "political" advisers and "consultants". With greater transparency and accountability, a variety of avenues are now available to citizens in obtaining information and/or redress. A devolution of personnel practices and conditions have occurred, together with the decentralization of budget responsibilities and, crucially, e-government.

THE DRIVING FORCES OF CHANGE

Key driving forces of change includes the new expectations that society at large have regarding governance, globalization, competitiveness and austerity in public spending. In addition, advances in telecommunications and information technology, and new trends in public sector management in developing and developed countries have also helped in influencing change. Also important is increased participation in economic and political decision-making.

Globalization has also changed the ways in which states manage their affairs. This has led to economic liberalization and the changing premises concerning competition, productivity, profitability and efficiency. The nature of market-based economics has challenged governments to become more open, responsive and, in many instances, more democratic. Inefficiencies in state organs have also raised questions about the functions of government. Increasingly, technological innovation and knowledge-based production require a better-educated and skilled work force, modern infrastructure, and adaptable and responsive private and public sector organizations.

In the words of Peter Drucker, "...the nation-state will survive the globaliisation of the economy and the Information Revolution that accompanies it. But it will be a greatly changed nation-state".

Here the public service sector faces a conundrum. The search for a new model for public service delivery is important, which would include the construction of new structures, systems and processes, including innovative ways of involving the private and voluntary sectors. Models that have been advanced include the New Public Management (NPM), civil service reforms, Re-inventing the Government, Re-engineering and Public Governance.

Most importantly, the new organization must have the following characteristics: it must be flexible and free flowing; it must be non-hierarchical; it must be based on participation; it must be creative and entrepreneurial; it must be based around networks driven by corporate concerns rather than narrowly defined functional solutions. Furthermore, it must utilize IT as a key resource and must involve a remoulding into a learning organization.

In Brunei, the roles of the public service sector are defined as follows: it is a provider of public goods and services; it is a facilitator of national growth and development; and it also plays a socio-economic role as a stabilizer.

The ideal civil servant should also possess several core qualities that the public service sector needs in order to perform at its best. He or she should be enterprising and customer-focused; transformational and visionary rather than reactionary and also innovative and creative; and should also be an empowered risk taker and leader for change, who is concerned more with output and outcome than processes. The ideal civil servant also knows the importance of being eagle-eyed, thus not seeing things in terms of segregated issues alone, and should be strategically inclined, multifunctional, a knowledge worker and also a team worker.

CONCERNS IN PUBLIC SERVICE

The concerns in the public service sector can be divided into two major areas. Firstly, there are traditional concerns that centre on efficiency, effectiveness and economy. Secondly, there are contemporary concerns, such as methods for dealing with the consumer age, the competitive age and the information age. In the consumer age, a more diverse public with a wider experience of different providers will demand better quality, more choices and higher standards. In this competitive age, issues such as regionalism and globalization have become increasingly relevant. It has become important to focus on harnessing technology as a factor of production. Changing management and on-demand skills have also become a crucial consideration. In addition, the knowledge economy (k-economy) and the knowledge worker (k-worker) have become issues to consider as well.

Consequently, HRD has become a major concern. For example, how do HRD programmes add value and competitiveness to the organization? How do HRD programmes exert an impact on the intellectual capital of an organization? How can investments in HRD programmes be directly related to sustainable organizational growth? Finally, do we know what the economic impact of using HRD programmes is? These concerns need serious consideration.

With regards to current HRD practices, it must be noted that many training opportunities are intended to remedy known or reasonably assumed skill or knowledge deficiencies. However, we must be conscious of the fact that it is easier to label problems as training problems than to look for the underlying factors behind deficiencies. Often, training is offered without the benefit of a diagnosis. Such phenomena put added focus on the need to switch from the tactical to the strategic. This means a switch to vision-based training programmes. Strategies also need to link training with corporate needs and organizational performance. Furthermore, there is a need to strategize in accordance with HRD aims. A framework for capacity building should be worked out and key elements for HRD framework based on current and future needs identified.

WHY STRATEGIC HRD?

The quality of our workforce determines the level to which we can set organizational objectives and the probabilities of success in achieving these objectives. Furthermore, the growth rate of an organization is likely to be limited more by its personnel than by any other factor. In an era of fast changes, technological advances and increased customer-orientation, the competitive edge of an organization depends on its strategic use of people.

There are numerous challenges for HRD in the public service sector. One is the creation of a competent and competitive workforce. Another is the transformation of the mindset of workers in the public service sector. HRD also needs to anticipate and identify future training needs. Furthermore, delivering practical knowledge and skills that are transferable to the workforce is also required. In short, HRD needs to be part of the whole strategic process.

Obstacles hampering the transformation of the HRD function in the public service sector must also be taken into account. Importantly, the most formidable of these is the lack of capability among human resource professionals. The second major obstacle lies within the top management itself.

WHEREFORE HRD IN THE PUBLIC SERVICE SECTOR?

An awareness of HRD as a key management tool is very much required. Furthermore, a linkage of HRD to the broader HR and organizational framework, namely a framework within which HRD activities can be planned and organized, should be constructed. Assessments of HRD within the context of organizational effectiveness as a whole should be carried out regularly.

CONCLUSION

The primary function of the public service sector is to translate national visions into tangible outcomes. This requires a clear articulation of the national vision as well as adequate resources. Effective partnerships between state organizations and the people are also vital in this respect. Also required is the ability of the managerial leadership to realize these visions.

Equally important is a competent and competitive workforce. Thus, the primary function of HRD programmes is to develop a long-term strategy for economic development and diversification, which will also create a competitive and innovative workforce. Such programmes must support processes of growth and diversification, as well as ensure that there are skilled and competent Bruneians available to continuously manage the process.

6

Human-focused Management for Future Progress

Chartchai Na Chiangmai

For some years, I have witnessed the increasing sense of international spirit and partnership that translates into important conventions. I believe the ASEAN-EC International HRD Convention is becoming a successful model for international cooperation. Since human capital development is a most important key to competitiveness and sustainable growth, cooperation between ASEAN and EC can be crucial to the development of human resource in ASEAN countries and beyond. It can inspire governments, business organizations, and civil society organizations to better ways of developing human resource and organizations. ASEAN-EC cooperation in human resource development should be congratulated on its past successes and is to be encouraged.

CHANGING PUBLIC SECTOR CONTEXTS AND PRIVATE MANAGEMENT IN ASEAN

A critical question confronting executives of private and public sector organizations in ASEAN countries today is not whether to change in response to their swiftly changed environment, but precisely how to manage that change. How do they modify organizational cultures and structures, and develop new capabilities to effectively cope with new challenges and uncertainties?

How, in particular, do they develop the human resource of their organizations to build up competitive capabilities for future progress and sustainable growth? What does it take for private and public organizations to succeed at human resource development?

This chapter begins with a new set of assumptions underlying the current economic, social, technological environment. Through this concept of changing realities, new capabilities of organizations and human resource in ASEAN countries can be identified. A key management strategy towards sustainable competitive capability is proposed. The chapter outlines a model for human-focused management to create new capabilities. The Siam Cement Group of Thailand is a case study of a successful organization that gives high priority to human resource development. The chapter ends with a brief discussion of organizational, structural and cultural constraints on human resource development.

A future trend of the world is the inclusion of all people under the rule of free competition. Many recent books point out that we are becoming inevitably more interdependent in making decisions and choosing our path to sustainable development (Handy 1994, Naisbitt 1994, Castells 1996, Huntington 1998, and Drucker 1999). This new concept leads to a change in basic economic and social assumptions:

- From economic independence to interdependence of people, communities, nations, and the world;
- From social fragmentation to social networks;
- From political and administrative to horizontal linkage;
- Centralization Distributed Governance; and
- From Single Objective/Single to Multiple objectives/multi-purpose organizations.

The current economic, business, social and political situations in ASEAN have apparently already confirmed these changes.

Globalization, democratization and the increasingly interconnected world have brought about new social values and an unprecedented volume of demands and expectations on citizens and consumers, where the performance of the public and private sectors in ASEAN countries are concerned. Private and public sector organizations are facing similar pressures. They are in the midst of a global institutional transformation. They have to renew management values and principles to respond effectively to new external challenges. More importantly, they have to increase rapidly their adaptive and learning capabilities to become more competitive.

Globalization has increasingly weakened the capabilities of the public sector in responding effectively and in a timely manner to complex and diverse demands. Existing laws, regulations and, government programmes and services have become less functional, if not irrelevant, relative to new situations and needs. Prevailing social norms and practices seem unable to provide a proper understanding of, and to solve, new versions of old problems. Many governments have difficulties in conceptualizing and steering their actions effectively in areas such as international trade, international security and counter-terrorism, and prevention of communicable diseases.

The free flow of communication and capital has also created more diversified niche markets and intensified business competition in ASEAN. Now that China and India are rising from their economic slumber that had lasted for over two centuries, two business trends in ASEAN are observable. First, the number for joint ventures and mergers of big businesses in ASEAN countries is growing, mainly to increase competitive advantages. Second, small and medium enterprises (SMEs), making up approximately 90% of ASEAN's economy, are forced to find new capabilities and competitiveness. Product development, new value creation and proactive marketing are main issues of discussion and research.

Central to the challenges encountered by the public and private sectors is change management. It is the question of how best an organization should manage changes so that it becomes an innovative and adaptive organization. The ability to generate new ideas and new knowledge as well as to increase the speed of learning in and between organizations is the key to future progress.

ASEAN governments have found that conventional ideas and modes of development administration are becoming less appropriate. Responsive government appears to be an important priority. Citizen-focused government and managing for results are two central themes of public service reforms in the region. Similarly, executives and managers of business firms in the region have relentlessly sought to find big ideas to achieve higher productivity and growth in order to increase long-term shareholder value. Innovation and differentiation are widely adopted as two key business strategies. The so-called management paradigms of make-to-sell and command-and-control have been replaced by those of sense-and-response and empowerment. Outside-in management is being given more attention than the inside-out version.

Strategy setting and effective implementation of strategy for value creation are of utmost importance to both private and public organizations. The New Economy and social assumptions and management paradigms also suggest that management strategies should have multiple goals in order to reach a balanced development within the organizations and their surrounding ecology. In this regard, knowledge and knowledge management are important factors for effective strategic planning and management.

The ability of an organization to develop people and manage knowledge has much to do with the competitiveness and sustainable development of the organization. As experience and knowledge contributing to competitiveness is mainly tacit, a common theme permeating most definitions of successful products or service delivery suggests that human-focused management is and will always be a most important priority of the organizations.

The central message is clear that human-focused management, together with collaborative knowledge management across all stakeholders in the organizational ecology, will produce results for the customers. These results include the effective management and delivery of products and services.

Private and public sector organizations in ASEAN therefore have to possess more capabilities to (1) conceive and execute complex strategies; (2) acquire, share, and protect intellectual capital, particularly indigenous wisdom; and (3) manage the interaction of networks of interests and forces in society to the best benefit of the organization and those in the ecology.

For policy-makers and business executives, the task is to sustain current capabilities while simultaneously building those required for tomorrow's success. To do this, organizations and people must learn to be ambidextrous. Thus, the ability to learn from existing results and experiences in order to leap forward to new and superior performance is indeed challenging.

What management and strategy should be brought into use to build these capabilities?

The adaptability of organizations in a knowledge-based economy and society needs a management strategy that is identical to the structural pattern of changes happening in social, economic, and political life. To be successful in the networked world, organizations and people should be organized and managed around a management strategy that fosters the ability to be more productive and to learn fast.

In the context of new socio-economic and political paradigms and the required competitive capabilities for organizations and people mentioned above, effective managers cannot focus only on know-how and know-why but know-who as well. Mastery of each individual or human capital is not enough. Connections that link individuals or units into a community or social capital are very important too. For effective organizations, the economics of connection is becoming as important as the economy of speed. In this sense, the free and quick flow of communication through connections is essential for collective learning and for increasing the speed of learning.

In this conceptualization, "link and learn" is the key strategy for a human-focused management to build up competitive capabilities.

Management itself is, in fact, a living system. It is based more on biological principles than physical principles. We should apply our understanding of biological systems to the design of structures and processes of relationships between people, communities, and nations. The structure of a biological system is characterized by networks of relationships. They are complex, diverse, and interdependent sets of relationships or sub-systems. Each sub-system is capable of self-organizing and adapting to the changing environment. They do this by linking to and learning from other sub-systems (Barabasi 2003). We should use this evolutionary biological process to drive our ideas and actions in developing people and organizations.

To implement the "link and learn" strategy effectively, I here suggest a model of human-focused management. From the perspective of managing change and development, the model should be based on the congruence of important management factors. The three main components of human-focused management are as follows:

1. Organizational architecture
2. Human resource development
3. Management philosophy and culture

1. Organizational Architecture

An agile organization able to leap from strength to strength needs a capability to do well in external adaptation and internal integration. To do this, an organization needs a redesign of organizational structure based on a concept of network management and a renewal of work processes in line with a coordination of productivity and growth strategy, function integration, and empowerment (PFE).

In networked organizations, horizontal linkages are more important and meaningful than vertical relations. Organizations and people are tied together by shared vision, shared purpose, and collective commitment. While power and authority flow vertically, information and knowledge flow and grow horizontally. The effectiveness of network management is based on trust and communication. Only when we trust each other, dp we listen and learn from each other.

Linking people and organizations through structures and processes is not enough to ensure an increase in the speed of learning and in the level of learning capabilities. We need a management principle that not only enhances knowledge management but also facilitates the use of knowledge to improve organizational performance. The principle is the coordination of productivity and growth strategy, functional integration, and empowerment (PFE). This coordination principle provides a firm ground for effective implementation of the organizational strategies. It enhances and supports self-learning and collective learning of cross-functional teams and self-managed teams.

Through processes of developing a holistic understanding of current organizational contexts and formulating productivity and growth strategies, executives and team members are together realizing which functions, activities or resources should be integrated into a single whole in implementing strategies to achieve business goals and objectives. With proper external and internal linkages and empowerment, employees, particularly at the lower levels, will unleash their potential and capabilities to work and learn to the fullest. The best guarantee for the development of the staff is to trust them and give them self-confidence, opportunity and appropriate resources.

2. Human Resource Development

For an effective human-focused management, a concept of human resource development promoting a continuous learning process in the organization is necessary. Human resource development here refers to an interactive process of enhancing and facilitating the development of capabilities and potential of individuals, organizations, and communities, through knowledge management, organizational development, and community development, to attain personal goals and organizational as well as communal goals effectively, efficiently, and harmoniously.

This definition suggests that a concept of human resource development should include at least four key elements:

- Interactive learning through action to develop capabilities and potential.
- Learning process should take place within the organizational and communal contexts.
- Learning activities should be effective, efficient and harmonious.
- Personal goals as well as those of organizations and communities should be simultaneously attained.

The concept suggests that one should bear in mind three different perspectives of management in developing human resource. Human resource development is a holistic and developmental process:

- It is the process of balancing internal and external views or balancing inside-out and outside-in perspectives.
- Developing human resource in organizations successfully requires both structural intervention and psycho-cultural adaptation.
- Linkages between three levels of development, i.e., the individual, the organization, and the community, should be properly steered and facilitated.

3. Management Philosophy and Culture

The competitive capabilities of organizations and people cannot be sustained if the human-focused management and human resource development mentioned above is not guided by a well-defined and powerful management philosophy and learning culture. Organizational culture is the system of shared actions, values, and beliefs that develops within an organization and guides the behaviour of its members (Schein 1990). The culture of an organization can have an important impact on its performance and its members' quality of work life.

Competitive organizations in ASEAN need to create a collective experience of their members to cope effectively with two important survival issues — external adaptation and internal integration.

External adaptation is concerned with achieving goals and interacting with outsiders. Through processes of interactive actions and collective learning, members will develop a common purpose, a mission, values and responsibility, and methods of coping with success and failure. At Siam Cement Group, for example, employees believe that it is their responsibility to innovate and contribute creatively.

Internal integration involves creating a collective identity and finding ways of matching methods of working and living together. Through dialogue and interaction, employees will shape up their own unique identity, community and their world and their understanding and acceptance of individual and group capabilities, performance, and rewards. Executives of the Siam Cement Group in the past few years have strived for real progress through innovation and differentiation by making themselves and the employees believe that together they can change their world, and what appears to be a crisis is in fact an opportunity for progress.

While structure and strategy are required for the building of strong foundations for a high performance organization, organizational culture has to be managed to serve as a guiding beacon. Executives and managers of private and public organizations reinforce an existing strong culture and build new cultures in required situations and areas. Krames (2003) gives examples of how the seven best CEOs in the United States brought new and fresh approaches to transform successfully the culture and performance of their businesses. What these CEOs did in common was that they led their organizations with a powerful management philosophy. They turned their organizations into principle-centred ones.

A principle-centred organization possesses a resilient management philosophy that gives an ethical and cultural basis for the members to develop and connect goals and strategies with capabilities and resources, which subsequently brings about effective ways of managing relationships and activities.

It can be noted that business development in many countries in this region over the past four decades has been primarily driven by economic theories and concepts of business management that put a relatively strong emphasis on ideas and techniques of business value adding. Little attention has been given to the discussion and application of management philosophy that links strategies of growth, profitability and customer service with indigenous Asian values and attitudes.

The 1997 economic crisis resulting from the collapse of leading business firms taught Thailand the costly lesson that sustainable business growth cannot be achieved without a crystal-clear and powerful management philosophy serving as a foundation for knowledge-building, values, and beauty of development.

One such management philosophy is based on the philosophy of sufficiency economy bestowed to the Thai people by His Majesty King RAMA IX, the present monarch of Thailand. The philosophy of sufficiency economy has been kindly bestowed to the Thai people by the King over the past 30 years. The philosophy can be observed and learned through many royal development initiatives and programmes. The philosophy was voiced strongly to the Thais again right after the economic crisis in 1997.

The philosophy of sufficiency economy has its intellectual origins in Buddhism and Asian values and attitudes towards life and the world. It embraces a set of guiding principles towards achieving human security and sustainable human development as well as societal and business development.

Sufficiency economy is a system of morals and values for decent living and righteous behaviour for people of all walks of life, from family, community all the way up to the state. Development of the economy and the running of business should be conducted on the principle of the middle path to cope effectively with uncertainties and risks. Sufficiency refers to having enough, being rational, and having good self-protection systems to withstand the impact of external and internal changes. In doing so, one must be omniscient or well informed, circumspect, and very careful in applying various knowledge and sciences to every step of the planning and implementation process. In the meantime, the morality of the people, especially government officials, theorists, and businessmen of every echelon, must be reinforced to raise consciousness about honesty, patience, perseverance, and right-mindedness so that they are ready to respond to swift global changes.

The philosophy of sufficiency economy is at the heart of Thailand's ninth national economic and social development plan. Public and private organizations as well as community organizations are studying and applying this philosophy to their businesses and situations. The Siam Cement Group is a principle-centred organization that has brought the philosophy of sufficiency economy into use in business operations.

The Siam Cement Group (SCG) is the biggest conglomerate in Thailand. SCG has been a major force in building Thailand's industry strength and know-how. It was founded in1913 by His Majesty King RAMA VI to engage in cement manufacturing and distribution. It has since diversified to meet the needs of Thailand's growing economy, establishing and participating in new industries, as warranted by technology and market demand. At present, Siam Cement has six core businesses, i.e., paper, petrochemicals, cement, building products, ceramics, and distribution, and two holding companies. It has been widely recognized in this region as a high performance business group characterized by good business performance, good return on equity and good social responsibility, together with a strong business philosophy and professionalism. SCG has received many excellence awards in productivity and quality management both at the regional and domestic levels (For more information, see www.siamcement.com).

An ongoing study conducted by Kusumawalee on the management philosophy and culture of SCG found that the group has been highly successful mainly because it is a principle-centred organization. With strong commitment to a well-established business philosophy, it can be considered not only as a high performance organization, but an adaptive and living organization as well. After having some financial problems during the economic crisis in 1997, Siam Cement began the twenty-first century as a restructured and refocused group of companies capable enough to be leaders in their respective industries. SCG possesses four important organizational attributes that studies have found common to successful business organizations (Senge 1985, Zook 2004):

- Adherence to fairness;
- Belief in the value of the individual;
- Concern for social responsibility;
- Dedication to excellence.

These principles are summarized in two words "Quality and Fairness". They are the breeding ground for the company's business ethics and practice. These management principles have been employed within the Siam Group for so many years that they have now become its corporate culture.

The business philosophy and culture of the Siam Group is in accordance with the philosophy of sufficiency economy and can be observed in some aspects of management practice.

Over the past decades, top executives of SCG have expressed themselves as good role models of leadership to the employees. Their behaviour at work has been very much in line with SCG management principles. They are persons with honesty, integrity, responsibility, self-discipline, a hard-working attitude, and strong sense of professionalism.

The board of directors consists of highly experienced professionals from various occupational backgrounds with strong leadership and vision as well as ethical integrity. They have not only steered the company rightly and in a productive direction but also assured that their policies and decisions are in line with good business ethics and corporate governance.

Human resource policies and programmes based on the belief in the value of the individual and the idea of internal labour market or promotion from within have encouraged SCG to recruit aggressively the best and the brightest persons and to maintain them through well-designed systems of training and development as well as fair and sufficiently attractive compensation schemes.

At SCG, the staff is considered the most important of all assets. Continuous learning by individual employees and knowledge management activities have been strongly encouraged and supported within and between the group's companies. The human resource policy focused on people has in a way functioned as a reproduction system for the organization's culture. Generations of employees have been continuously socialized to align SCG's management philosophy and principles with that of their own.

Throughout its 90 years in operation, SCG has been relentless in its pursuit of excellence. Making the best and most efficient use of organizational resources, SCG in the past years has received many international awards recognizing its achievements in high labour productivity and total quality management. Asia's Best Companies 2003 and Deming Application Prize from the Union of Japanese Scientists and Engineers are among its awards.

SCG has shown its deep concern for social responsibility by operating businesses with a strong sense of citizen duty and responsibility. The group has been involved in many developmental programmes dedicated to the conservation of natural resources and community development. The Siam Cement Foundation was set up to organize and provide support to educational and recreational activities as well as other philanthropic affairs in and outside the group's locations.

ORGANIZATIONAL STRUCTURE AND CULTURAL CHALLENGES TO SUCCESSFUL HUMAN RESOURCE DEVELOPMENT

There are some organizational structural and cultural constraints on the application of human-focused management and the concept of human resource development proposed in this chapter. Many organizations in this region are organized in a highly centralized structure with inside-out perspectives of management, and a patronage style of leadership. In these organizations, rules and regulations are rather inflexible and employees favour defensive routines and exercise change resistance.

Such an organizational structure, management mindset and leadership style do not support the free flow of ideas and information within and between levels of organizational hierarchy. Cross-functional learning and collective or shared experience leading to innovation are less likely to be effective. Many employees whose jobs are relatively secure may feel complacent. They are in their comfort zone and are likely to resist change programmes.

Since learning and sharing knowledge with other organizations in the business ecology and/or community is increasingly important for human resource development, managers will face difficulties in facilitating learning and building knowledge in and between organizations in which information and knowledge as well as power and status are distributed asymmetrically. Since the competitiveness of an organization is more likely to be determined by the speed of learning, we need more research to gain a better picture of the know-how and the know-who that can make organizations learn fast in order to stay alive and well in the world of increasing uncertainties and risks.

REFERENCES

Barabasi, Albert-Laszlo. *Linked*. New York: Penguin Group, 2003.

Castells, Manuel. *The Rise of the Network Society*. Oxford: Blackwell, 1996.

Drucker, Peter F. *Management Challenges for the 21st Century*. New York: HarperCollins Publisher, 1999.

Handy, Charles. *The Age of Paradox*. Boston, Mass.: Harvard Business School Press, 1994.

Huntington, Samuel. *The Clash of Civilization and the Remaking of World Order*. London: Touchstone, 1998.

Krames, Jeffrey A. *What the Best CEOs Know*. New York: McGraw-Hill, 2003.

Kusumawalee, Sombat. "Application of the Philosophy of Sufficiency Economy in the Business Sector: A Case Study of the Siam Cement Group". Bangkok: National Institute of Development Administration. (Forthcoming).

Naisbitt, John. *Global Paradox: The Bigger the World Economy, the More Powerful its Smallest Players*. New York: William Morrow, 1994.

Schien, Edgar. "Organizational Culture", *American Psychologist*, Vol. 45 (1990): 109–19.

Senge, Peter. *The Fifth Discipline*. Boston: MIT Press, 1985.

Zook, Chris. *Beyond the Core*. Boston: Harvard Business School Press, 2004.

HRD STRATEGIES FOR COMPANIES

7

Crafting and Implementing a Strategic HR Programme

Roberto de Ocampo

Human resources or as some would call it, human capital, is becoming the most important asset for most organizations in the world. As the New Economy pervades the world's communities and organizations, it becomes necessary to study and pay close attention to the impact of globalization and technology in shaping today's strategy for managing human resources.

As a practitioner and student of human resource management, among other things, I believe that the globalization and the advancement of technology influence how organizations react and adjust to the changing times and economy.

Here, I would like to discuss the impact of the New Economy as well as its implications for today's global organizations. These factors necessitate specific responses and strategic moves from corporate, social, and country organizations to craft an optimal human resource strategy.

GLOBALIZATION AND ITS IMPACT ON ORGANIZATIONS

The first step in creating a human resource strategy in the New Economy is to take into consideration the effects of globalization and technological advancement on organizations.

The first noticeable effect is that the business environment has become more competitive as local companies compete with global players. As more companies compete in the same industry, customers are given more choices. With an increasing number of choices, customers are becoming more sophisticated and demand best-quality products and services at the lowest possible price.

Second, as the business landscape becomes more competitive, organizations have to be more efficient in their operations and strive for innovation in research and development. For companies to survive and grow in a dynamic and highly volatile marketplace, they must possess more flexibility, responsiveness and speed in marketing their products.

Third, in order to achieve organizational flexibility and responsiveness organizations need to create alliances with partners and suppliers, and foster innovation among its employees. The challenge in creating alliances lies in determining how to promote cooperation and mutual trust. Cooperation and mutual trust, within the organization and throughout its partner firms, are only possible if an organization is able to harmonize and synthesize the various cultures among its employees, suppliers and partners, blend eastern philosophy with western paradigms, or merge local customs with foreign practices.

Fourth, while globalization fosters intense competition, the advancement in technology has created a new breed of employees — more educated and knowledgeable, more innovative, and more mobile. This new breed of employees, considered as knowledge workers, are in turn invested upon by organizations as human capital. As such, they seek reasonable returns to investment and greater value in terms of personal development and professional advancement.

The challenge is really to understand the role of human resource management in an organization competing in a global business environment, and effectively define the critical issues and responses necessary in implementing a strategic programme.

ORGANIZATIONAL AND HUMAN RESOURCE CHALLENGES

If organizations are to survive and grow in a global business environment, they must respond by building a responsive organization, fostering innovation, and sustaining organizational capability.

Strategy I: Building Organizational Responsiveness through a Learning Organization

To build a responsive organization, firms must become more efficient. Efficiency means rationalizing and streamlining business processes. Streamlining business processes means new work modalities for employees. For new work modalities to be implemented, an organization has to upgrade the competencies and skills of its employees.

While organizational efficiency calls for a rationalization of business processes within the firm, it also necessitates employees to work with people from partner companies that have different cultural and organizational backgrounds. The role of human resource management, therefore, is to create cultural literacy. This means providing employees with training on cultural sensitivity, cross-functional work relations, and strategic direction. Cultural literacy is critical in making alliances work in the way top management intends it to. Accomplishing this allows employees and allied partners to think on the same wavelength and thus respond more intelligently and efficiently to the demands of the New Economy.

Second, as business processes are streamlined, it becomes important for companies to harvest knowledge across the organization. Harvesting knowledge means codifying information, knowledge and experience and to leverage these for organizational learning. Knowledge sharing helps build organizational capability and responsiveness by creating an employee mindset that is customer-focused, updated and dynamic. A major challenge, however, in harvesting knowledge is the employees' resistance to change. Employees may resist new modalities of work processes or may be hesitant to share knowledge and experiences with other members of the organization.

Third, as organizational processes change, the upgrade and development of skills become imperative. Changes in business processes require an upgrade in competencies to ensure the integration of skills creation with technological advancement. In the complex and fast moving workplace, human resource management must ensure that all employees are well trained, work seamlessly with each other, and have access to technology tools.

Strategy II: Building an Innovative Organization through Service Assets

Globalization and advances in technology have given rise to knowledge-based economies and have redefined the basis of competitive advantage. Physical resources such as production equipment and facilities have become less important compared to service assets such as competencies, goodwill and patents. The creation of service assets in the knowledge economy requires a new set of competencies that are more creative, proactive and entrepreneurial. Moreover, the creation of service assets entails the development of knowledge workers who are more creative and innovative. As Alexander Fliaster, who wrote on the Development of Knowledge Workers, has noted, in the knowledge economy, competencies have shifted from relatedness, interdependence and harmony to that of individuality, independence and self-responsibility. The focus has shifted from generalists to professionals or knowledge workers with distinctive, market-related skills and values.

In this regard, human resource management must then focus on developing creativity, individuality and entrepreneurship among employees as opposed to the traditional model of consistency, hierarchy and seniority. Companies must create a work atmosphere where distinctive personalities, non-traditional experience, and talented individuals are greatly appreciated. In the knowledge-based economy, it is the employees who become the investment that creates an organization's competitive advantage.

Second, while creativity and innovation are crucial for competitive advantage, the creation of organizational trust is also important. Trust is important in promoting innovation within the organization. The role of human resource management, therefore, is to strike a balance between promoting intellectual elites and high performers and securing loyalty and commitment from consensus-seeking employees. The challenge is to balance organizational unity with diversity, and homogeneity and conformity with proactiveness and flexibility.

Strategy III: Sustaining Organizational Capability through Talent Management and Retention

Lastly, if companies are to move forward and respond well to globalization, they must develop strategies to sustain long-term organizational capability. Sustaining capability has become an issue in the knowledge economy because of higher workforce mobility. Workforce mobility is a result of employees who are more informed, more aware of their choices and of their importance in the organization. Technology through the Internet also adds to workforce mobility by disseminating information on employment options and opportunities. An informed workforce in the New Economy understands its role as talents and human capital in business, and demands return for their investment.

To retain knowledge workers and sustain organizational capability, companies may choose to adopt several strategies in talent retention and management. For instance, companies may diversify contract forms for its knowledge workers. In lieu of the traditional longer-term contracts, companies may opt to employ yearly contracts. This arrangement allows organizations to attract professionals with creative ability, and at the same time provide them with employment flexibility and mobility. This type of arrangement is appropriate for technology companies, or for organizations that want to enter new markets where creative and entrepreneurial competencies are important.

Another option is to diversify the professional experience of knowledge workers into master degrees, mid-careers, foreign researchers, temporary hired contracts, and various industry backgrounds. The diversity of experience and industry background among employees will provide the impetus for innovation and creativity.

The third option is to diversify the recruitment criteria for knowledge workers. The objective is to balance the traditional recruitment criteria focused on relatedness and interdependence with that of individuality, originality and creativity. For instance, this strategy is useful for software companies where innovation and speed in marketing products are key competitive advantages.

A fourth strategy is to modify compensation packages in order to retain the most innovative knowledge workers and to allow an organization to foster job performance based on meritocracy.

Lastly, companies can diversify the schools and universities from which they recruit new employees. This system ensures a heterogeneous workforce and recruitment of talents with unconventional academic backgrounds.

ROLE OF HUMAN RESOURCE MANAGEMENT

In summary, what then is the role of human resource management in addressing the imminent trends affecting global organizations? The goal of human resource management in the New Economy must be three-fold:

1) To build an adaptive organization with a responsive workforce;
2) To build an innovative workforce that values creativity rather than commonality, and;
3) To manage and retain talents through diversification of workforce engagements.

An organization's human resource management must address the organization's needs for market responsiveness, innovation and organizational capability if it is to survive the ever-changing landscapes of the New Economy.

ROLE OF *IT* IN HUMAN RESOURCE MANAGEMENT

There is a need for the private sector to invest more in information technology for its human resources to meet new challenges posed by globalization, wherein local companies are finding themselves increasingly pitted against international players.

For the public sector, IT should be introduced at a young age to schoolchildren and the education curriculum should be attuned to the standards of the New Economy, starting with the cultivation of communication skills in English and the youths' exposure to cultures beyond their native soil.

8

Enhancing Human Capital in the New Economy

David Scruggs

Change is currently occurring at an unprecedented rate. The very speed of change in itself has tremendous implications not only for the business world, but also for the management of resources, especially human resources. Nowadays, business organizations are constantly hearing "more, better and faster with less" as the demand of the day. Focus should therefore be put on the link between rapid advances in technology and the way information and knowledge can both be harnessed and rendered obsolete in a short time.

Due to changes in the world environment, certain common trends in human resources are noticeable. Large companies, including government and big organizations, have to react quickly to stay competitive in today's world. The larger the company, the more difficult it is to be agile. There is also a growing need to manage the increased access to information through the Internet, since more information is available to everyone today. Access to information in turn changes the culture and diversity of work. Ultimately, as a result of this, there is an increasing need for *continuous learning* on everyone's part, if they are to remain competitive and relevant in today's burgeoning economy.

The development of human resources needs to take into account the various forces that are at play in today's dynamic world. In today's business reality, we frequently hear about the urge to have more things, to have better versions of them, to attain them at a faster rate, and to get them at lower costs. These are the result of the inevitable changes that are taking place everywhere. Furthermore, it is not just *change* itself that is the challenge. More importantly, it is the *speed* at which these changes take place that is making *change* itself more prominent. "The amount of time to double our knowledge in many fields has gone from being measured by centuries to being measured in months". Hence, employers and employees alike have to take into account the urgency of remaining relevant in an ever-changing environment. Human resource management thus has to consider addressing people who resist change; more precisely, those who resist *being changed.*

In order to encourage people — especially employees — to support some form of change, they must first play a part in the changes themselves, and to do so they must be given opportunities for change. It is more often likely that people will *support* a change in which they themselves have played a role in shaping. The fact is that one cannot empower people, but instead, empowerment is something that people *take*, provided they are in the right environment and in the right setting.

The changes that we see today have bearing on many aspects of human resource development, training and education. In the drive for continuous learning, empowerment, competitiveness and relevance, all things and all changes become pertinent. There is a continuous demand for new skills to be developed that run parallel with the speed of change, and there is a significant shift today from an emphasis on technical know-how to soft skills. Therefore the centrality of HRD should be in encouraging continuous learning, and not just occasional learning. This can certainly be done with today's tremendous improvements in access to information and mediums of delivery. People can do research with perceived ease, and can also do so in a cost-effective way. In a service-orientated business, research and knowledge are of vital importance. This is because if the customer or consumer knows more than we do or knows what is possible with our competitors, then this is a dangerous thing — someone once said: "nothing is more dangerous than an educated consumer".

Therefore, companies should strive not only for continuous improvements, but more importantly, for *breakthroughs*. While striving for continuous improvements involves looking into the past in order to improve things, looking at *breakthroughs* is a concept that winning companies adopt. To continue existing in a highly dynamic world, many companies often forget that *breakthroughs*, when made into a priority, can be a key component of their success. In the 1970s for instance, when the term *quality* became the buzzword, the definition was *conforming to requirements.* If things conformed, then they were high *quality.* Later this changed to *meeting consumer needs*, where quality alone was not enough. Now, the emphasis is on *exceeding customer expectations.* Organizations may want to ask *what is possible* or *what is impossible that I wish were possible*? Examples such as travelling with Richard Branson's airline, Virgin Atlantic, showed that the company had not only created breakthrough service, but also innovative ways that can certainly render other airline companies uncompetitive, since customers are beginning to get used to the fact that the impossible can indeed be done.

The concepts of innovation and breakthrough that are increasingly filtering into the domains of human resource development, management, and business practices, raise issues about good leadership. In this day and age, managers are expected to be leaders, coaches, and mentors at the same time. The question is — are they trained to be such? This is a new phenomenon that is affecting human resource management today. There is a need for entrepreneurial thinking, and there is a need for people to take risks and be good leaders. The issue then is how do we develop the people we have into the people that the company and we desire? There are a few steps that are important in addressing this issue, and more importantly, in tackling the *skills gap* that may exist between what I can do now and what I need to be doing in the future because of the rapidity of change. People and organizations have to gain proper leverage and balance themselves in three main areas — access to information, assets and environment. There are three areas — education, motivation and training — that need to be balanced to form a *Triangle of Performance*. To undergo processes of change, organizations have to go through the *Cycle of Change and Growth*.

People need to change and move or they will die just like if sharks do not move in the water they cannot breathe. All steps involve a change in attitudes. This in itself may be difficult because attitudes are very personal things. As a boss, one may *force* an employee to change, but as a leader, force may not be the most viable of ways. Many have tried to change but don't always succeed or be afraid of the change. Therefore, they must first *believe* that they can do it. For example, the smoker who is a habitual quitter may not believe he can stop. There is thus a motivation gap that needs to be overcome. Attitudes can be changed and developed but not by the same mindset that was there in the past. Though some managers or employees may not like it, a paradigm shift is needed. The appropriate knowledge and skills are also two other important aspects of change.

In conclusion, it is firstly important to note that real change requires a change in mindset. *Change* is an uncomfortable thing and creates stress. While some may be able to deal with stress, and others may even thrive on it, a significant percentage of people do not handle it well. Thus in HRD, stress management will be a big thing in the future. With the right tools, the right skills and ample knowledge, motivated individuals with the right coaching and right practices have a chance to make new and improved changes permanent.

9

Competency Development for Superior Performance

R. Palan

INTRODUCTION

Almost every company says people are the most important resource but everyone agrees that it is extremely difficult to put a tangible value on people's contribution towards the bottom line. The common sense acceptance that people do create shareholder value has been difficult to prove in the absence of data.

Management experts contend that only 30% of market capitalization is due to physical assets. This then leads to the question of what it is that contributes to the remaining 70%.

Recently, Watson Wyatt Worldwide, a global consulting firm, released its Human Capital Index. The study demonstrated the link between superior human resource practices and the creation of shareholder value. If and when an organization implements good practices in the six key areas mentioned below, then positive financial outcomes follow.

SIX KEY AREAS

1. Ensuring the competence of employees whether by acquisition, deployment or development;
2. Managing talent;
3. Providing clear rewards and accountability;
4. Maintaining communications integrity;
5. Prudent use of human resources, and;
6. Focused use of technology in HR.

Here, the first two areas will be reviewed.

Throughout the Asia HRD Congress, experts have spoken about ideas and action strategies revolving around global HRD learning strategies, HR measurement, quality of work life, talent development and competency management. We have also heard the age-old maxim that change is a constant feature in an organization's life.

As companies meet the challenges arising out of change, they have no choice but to focus on human capital, since that is the only source from which an organization can gain competitive advantage.

FOCUS ON HUMAN CAPITAL

Business success and organizational prosperity grow from employees performing at higher levels: learning on a continuous basis; being more process-oriented; leveraging existing knowledge; collaborating as a team; and being more responsible for creating value by creating knowledge that enhances an organization's competitive edge. Business success does not happen by accident. It happens by design.

At a time when lean organizations are forging partnerships to achieve their business strategy and maintain core values, the new competitive environment has serious implications for competency management and human capital management. HRD professionals now bear the responsibility for aligning individual and team behaviour with organizational behaviour and strategy. Though competency is not the sole cause of performance, it is a vital component for performance improvement.

In short, organizations need a competent workforce for success. This is a pre-requisite for building and retaining intellectual capital. We can safely conclude that knowledge is a scarce resource in an information-driven world. It must not be forgotten that this knowledge is mainly tacit; it rests in people's heads. When employees leave the organization, they walk away with the knowledge.

MANAGING COMPETENCIES IN AN ORGANIZATION

Are we able to manage the competencies of the organization? Can we store and share knowledge and ensure a decent return on investment? This chapter will include a case study, a best practice on how organizations can create a direct link between competency management and financial performance. Before we do that, let me paint a quick outline of the competency movement.

Competencies: Why the Need?

The English dictionary describes the word "competence" as suitable, fit, or sufficient. However, the words competence/competencies mean different things to different people. To create competencies, we need to find answers to the following questions:

1. Do we understand the meaning of the word competency?
2. Why do we as an organization want to create competencies?
3. What does the organization want to do with competencies and which of the following is the focus on?
   i.   Competency acquisition;
   ii. Competency development;
   iii. Competency deployment, and;
   iv. Competency management (talent management/succession planning/ knowledge management).

What Does the Word Competency Mean?

A clear understanding of the philosophy behind each concept is vital for successful competency creation.

1. Competence/s
This usually refers to surface competencies such as knowledge and skills. It is defined as the demonstration of knowledge and skills, and as a required standard in a given context to produce a product or service, and the ability to transfer knowledge and skills to a new and different context. These are usually referred to as functional competencies and generally refer to technical skills. Organizations in the UK, Australia, Malaysia, and the Middle East focus heavily on functional competence development.

2. Competencies
Originally introduced by Prof. McClelland, the term "competencies" usually refers to the underlying characteristics of an individual that is causally related to criterion-referenced effective and/or superior performance in a job/situation. This refers to a fairly deep and enduring part of a person's personality and can predict behaviour in a wide variety of situations and job tasks. "Causally related" means that a competency causes or predicts behaviour and performance. "Criterion-referenced" means that the competency actually predicts high performance or poor performance as

measured on specific criteria. This is usually referred to as behavioural competencies. Behavioural competencies focus on how an employee creates value and what the actual accomplishment is. In other words, a cluster of behavioural competencies (competency model focusing on superior performers) answers the question — "In a particular work setting, what does an excellent performer look like?"

3. Core competencies
Originally introduced by Gary Hamel and CK Prahalad, this refers to operational competencies that provide the organization with a competitive edge. These are bundles of skills or technologies that enable a company to provide a particular benefit to its customers. A core competency provides greater customer value, differentiation from competition and a gateway to the future.

4. Role competencies
These are usually linked to positions and also known as leadership or professional competencies. Generally behavioural in nature, they refer to the position's critical roles in developing performance and managing human capital.

WHY DO ORGANIZATIONS WANT TO CREATE COMPETENCIES?

Successful organizations are very clear about the need to create competencies. The need is usually derived from a positive correlation between social and economic needs. In the Middle East, organizations focus on competency development. The goal is to develop local talent to take over from the expatriate workforce.

Organizations wishing to operate in first world markets are forced to develop a competent workforce because of stringent quality certification requirements. This is so since a deficiency here resulting in withdrawal of quality accreditation would mean severe loss of business.

More immediate benefits include lower insurance premiums in high-risk industries when a competency system is in place. Residual risk profiles when calculating the likelihood of occurrence of a risk situation and the magnitude of impact require the presence of a competency system. Multi-skilling, the requirement for mobility, and continuous improvement targets, require employees to move up the performance gradient. Any performance improvement programme rests on a competency foundation, although the mere presence of a competent workforce does not guarantee performance. The presence of a coherent strategy to create competencies is a prerequisite for success.

THE FOCUS OF COMPETENCIES

If an organization understands the thought process behind the variety of competency approaches and has a business case for creating competencies, then the next question concerns organizational focus. Organizations have adopted one, a combination, or all of the approaches to create competencies.

- Competency acquisition — desired competencies that are needed but unavailable in the organization are mapped and acquired through recruitment.
- Competency development — developing the existing competency level of employees through sustained learning programmes.
- Competency deployment — deploying through multi-skilling and lateral people movement to meet just-in-time business requirements. Matching people to the right position is a critical application.
- Competency management — capturing, assessing and reporting the competency levels to ensure the business has the human capital to implement its strategy in the market. Talent Management, Succession Planning and Knowledge Management are some of the applications. Competency management is usually driven by a powerful database that records and reports competency information for applications.

Without a coherent business case, an understanding of the philosophy behind each concept, and a focus, it is impossible for a competency model to be built.

IMPLEMENTING COMPETENCIES

Project champions provide "contagion" leadership for successful implementation. Without them, it will be a futile effort to get line management support. Despite the widespread availability of generic competency dictionaries, line managers who are subject matter experts and who know more about organizational processes must support the implementation process.

Getting a job competency profile validated or the organizational job profile matrix endorsed is next to impossible without line manager support. The competency assessment of a jobholder poses a similar challenge.

A TEN-STEP PROCESS

To meet project timelines and gain line manager support for successful implementation, we at SMR follow a simple ten-step process:

1) Have a project plan with clear deliverables.
2) Form a project team that comprises predominantly of line managers.
3) Get the project champion to sell the benefits of competency management.
4) Have a full-time core implementation team dedicated to the project.
5) Establish the technology infrastructure before project commencement to ensure minimum slippage of time.
6) Establish regular reporting structure involving the project champion and the top management.
7) Implement change control procedures to ensure that any change has purpose and justification.
8) Avoid references to performance in any campaign.
9) Ensure that every deliverable when delivered is signed off.
10) Document the project systematically.

INSTITUTIONALIZING A COMPETENCY MANAGEMENT SYSTEM FOR SUPERIOR PERFORMANCE

For the system to outlast the implementation period and to become a mainstream operational tool there is a need to demonstrate the business benefits. Any economic gain or quick wins must be broadcast to the entire organization to legitimize the importance of competency management. This is a must for two reasons:

1) The economic value of competent superior performance is statistically defined as one standard deviation (SD) above average performance, roughly the level achieved by the top 1 person out of 10 in a particular work environment. The value of one SD above the mean is 19% to 48% output for non-sales jobs and 48% to 120% for sales jobs. The economic value of superior performance is a powerful return on investment for institutionalizing a competency management system.

A recent survey by Hay Consultants found superior sales people (average salary of US$41,777) sold an average of US$6.7 million while average performers sold an average of US$3 million. The superior group sold 123% more than the average sales people. The difference was worth not 120% but 8857% or 89 times the average salary. The data suggests the economic value of adding one superior performer to the team, which results in considerable returns.

2) Organizations should "apply" their knowledge of competencies in everyday processes. Recruitment templates, training systems driven by competency gaps, and competency-based performance systems embed competencies into everyday processes. Acquire the right competency sets, develop the required competencies, and measure competency growth. Failure to do so will result in selecting and training for mediocrity — the organization's current average level of performance.

CONVERTING INTENTIONS TO REALITY

Intel's Grove remarked: "When you come to a fork in the road you have to decide which direction to take, otherwise you risk hitting the divider".

The pace of change forces us to take action, do something about what we know. Change forces us to choose a direction. Organizations generally focus on numbers and objectives but in recent years, they have begun to realize that organizations do not achieve performance; it is people who produce results. Competencies are not another form of performance appraisals but as Intel's Grove said, they enable people to become the best they can be. GE's Jack Welch talked about developing a sense of stretch within people.

Every organization intends to develop a superior workforce to achieve superior performance. They also realize what Sumantra Ghosal and Christopher Bartlett have noted: "You cannot manage a third generation company with second generation processes with first generation employees". Employee competence acquisition, development, deployment, and management are necessary to convert noble intentions to ground realities — which is about survival in today's competitive times.

A BEST PRACTICE CASE STUDY

We had the opportunity of working on a consulting project with an international hotel chain. With service being the only differentiator, competency was a critical component of the service strategy. Believing in competency is one thing, and implementing a competency initiative within the chain with hotels dispersed geographically around the world, with different owners and multiple language requirements, is another. Our experience with the team in implementing a competency-based human resource system was delightful and full of learning experiences. The best part of the experience was the clear direction set by the top management.

The first interaction with them was an interesting one. They had a clear idea of what they wanted to gain through the implementation of a competency-based HR project. It was clear that a lot of thinking and discussion among the internal teams had preceded our meeting. The lack of clarity that is usually an impediment to the project was missing. The project team was very clear about its goals. The competency initiative had a clear project plan with clearly described deliverables.

Though the project team did not include many line managers, something that we usually prefer, it was communicated and sold to the line managers through the general managers. The nature of the hotel industry made it impossible to gather all the line managers for a briefing to communicate to them the benefits of the competency initiative. This worried us, as the insufficient involvement of the line is always a recipe for resistance to change. However the communication process was carried out through the hotel hierarchy in a structured manner.

The project champion systematically sold the benefits of the competency initiative to the top management, the general managers of each hotel and then to the human resources community within the hotel chain. Considerable care was taken to ensure that everyone was included in the communication loop to ensure a successful implementation. This was critical as the employees and the managers had to accept the competencies.

Though the positions were globalized to reflect standardization within the hotels distributed globally, care was taken to allow changes to meet the local situation.

The full-time project team was totally dedicated to the implementation of this project. This dedication helped to create a competency dictionary for the occupational groups within the hotel group. Though the occupational competencies and the behavioural ones were based on job families, the project team went to great lengths to receive feedback from the hotels about the local situation. For instance, in South Korea and Japan, the competencies were translated into the local language. Competencies relevant to the local situation and cultural factors were taken into consideration. The mammoth task involved a mass of data.

Usually we find the customer getting overwhelmed with the volume of data. However, in this situation, the dedicated project team was very meticulous and comfortable with the mass of data. This allowed them to carefully create and evaluate each occupational competency, the competency indicators and the evidence guide.

Each hotel's technology infrastructure was also evaluated well before the implementation date. The IT head in each hotel was involved with the implementation of the initiative. This ensured the minimum slippage of time with non-implementation areas.

Most importantly, a clear communication structure was agreed to between the members of the team, the reporting structure involving the project champion and the management was established, thereby ensuring continuous communication. This also guaranteed corporate visibility for the project team.

Any project of this nature will almost always involve changes. We agreed with the project team on a change control procedure. The purpose of having a change control procedure was to ensure that each and every change that comes about during the project period has a purpose and justification. The lack of one or an additional one that is more of an enhancement to the scope of the project usually delays the project.

In this project, every change was well thought out prior to implementation, user feedback was taken and eventually when it was put to us, it was not too difficult to see the validity for the change. Despite the changes the project team asked for, the project was one of the few where the number of changes from the original project scope document was insignificant. This simply proved that prior preparation goes a long way towards helping the implementation of a successful project.

The focus in this project was on development. The hotel environment included another additional player — the union. The communication process helped win its confidence and clearly prove to its leaders that the initiative was neither a right-sizing one nor was it one that would affect their compensation. On the contrary, it was introduced to make employees competent and successful in their jobs. The thought that this process was value adding helped win them over. One of the strategies used was to avoid reference to performance. This was to indicate that the project was not another performance appraisal. Hence all references to performance when creating position competency profiles were removed. For example, when the required level was described for a competency, the required level was termed as a required competency level rather than performance level.

Whenever project deliverables were achieved, the project team made it a point to communicate the achievement of the milestone to the rest. We do sometimes encounter reluctance from a client to sign off the completion of the stage and move to the next. Indecision leads to unnecessary delays. In line with project management principles, we do not move on to the next stage unless the earlier stage is signed off. With this project team, that was not an issue. The ability to move fast and at the same time carefully was certainly a positive attribute of the project team.

Just as we were about to conclude the project we received news that the project champion was about to leave the organization. It created worries since the lack of continuity could affect the success of the project. However, with the clear reporting structure, each stage had been clearly documented and there was no cause for concern as the carefully chosen successor had all the knowledge codified for easy knowledge sharing. It was not a case of the project champion walking away with the knowledge.

At this point, the organization has the following already in place:

- A standardized list of positions and jobs.
- A competency dictionary.
- Competency profiles for all positions.
- An assessor programme, though not a sophisticated one. The assessment is carried out by the employees themselves, their supervisors, and trained assessors.
- A competency gap analysis for each person, department and the organization.
- A global competency inventory into which the organization can tap for the purpose of internal recruitment.
- A training plan detailing all the development programmes needed to close the competency gaps.
- Development suggestions for each employee.
- Over 100 reports, including test results available for decision-making on succession planning and training management.
- A body of competency experts.
- Trained users of the system HRDPower.

THE DRIVER

HRDPower, the competency-based system, was implemented throughout the hotel chain. It helped streamline the implementation as well as make the initiative cost effective. The project was completed well ahead of time and under budget for an unbelievable cost. The focal points at each hotel were able to learn and drive the system and generate the reports needed for effective decision-making.

THE FUTURE

Although we can certainly call it a best practice, the project team thinks they have just started. They want to simulate team competencies and return on investment scenarios. They want to answer questions to management on areas such as the following: Does an increase in competency lead to an increase in performance? Does the additional investment on competency growth lead to at least a corresponding gain in performance? Can we prove value creation by isolating development actions from other variables? Can competency be integrated with the performance management system? Can we sustain the current line management interest?

These are some of the burning questions that the project team hopes to answer. The team is certainly not complacent about their initial win that they so successfully broadcasted to the world. They are working on the next phase to score the next win to add value to the organization and show that people do add value to the bottom line.

The learning from this best practice can be summarized in the following sentences: The necessity to ensure that the right person is in the right job is no longer a luxury but an issue of survival, and, prior preparation and a strong project champion are a must if the project is to be completed successfully.

* Communicate, communicate and communicate is a good maxim to follow.
* Dispersed locations are no longer an excuse, HRDPower allows you to connect with every location to create a competency inventory for the organization.
* Have a project plan and sell it to decision-makers.
* Reporting and documentation are critical components of the project.
* There needs to be a provision for sharing knowledge.
* Involve all levels to overcome resistance.
* Highlight the difference between competency assessment and performance appraisal.
* Track schedules and costs.

REFERENCES

Ghosal, Sumantra and Christopher Bartlett. *The Individualised Corporation*. Harper Business Books, 1999.

Hamel, Gary and C.K. Prahalad. *Competing for the Future*. Harvard Business School Press, 1994.

McClelland, David. *Testing for Competence rather than Intelligence*. American Psychologist, 1973.

Palaniappan, Ramanathan. *The SMR Viewpoint*. Specialist Management Resources, 1999.

Palaniappan, Ramanathan. *Competency Management: a business practitioner's guide*. Specialist Management Resources, 2003.

Sloan, S. and L.H. Spencer. "Hay Sales Force Participant Survey Results". Hay Management Consultants, 1991.

10

Leading with Emotional Intelligence

David Cory

ABSTRACT

To lead with emotional intelligence is to inspire, to motivate, to instill a sense of worth, belonging, confidence, and to compel others to work to their fullest potential. Successful leadership is measured by the emotions of others. How does one develop such leadership skills? Leadership experts seem to agree that it requires an inside-out approach to developing leaders. It becomes critical for leaders to increase their awareness of their ability to manage themselves and their relationships with others. Emotional intelligence appears to be in addition to cognitive intelligence, as measured by one's IQ, and not a component of it. To lead with emotional intelligence involves an examination of the foundational skills and competencies that underlie leadership competencies. It involves a thorough understanding of the component parts of emotional intelligence and how each one can be developed in the workplace for greater organizational effectiveness.

INTRODUCTION

Where are the leaders who inspire us, motivate us and make us feel that we can achieve great things? Where are the leaders who, when we are with them, give us a sense of self-confidence and self-worth, and we feel like we "belong"? Where are the leaders who make us *feel* good? We feel like we do our best work for leaders when we have these qualities. We do not want to leave leaders who make us feel these positive emotions. I suggest that leaders with these qualities are out there, but 1 think it is also safe to say the world could do with more of them. This paper will discuss the difference between leaders and managers and what skills need to be developed to create more leaders who are able to inspire workers for maximum organizational effectiveness.

LEADERS AND MANAGERS

Think about the managers that you have worked for in your career so far. They were all managers, but were they all leaders? What's the difference? "Manager" is usually the name of the position that we use to refer to the person that gets things done. They have a responsibility to ensure that those tasks that are within the scope of their job are completed. Thus, the manager manages people, things, budgets, resources, etc. to ensure that tasks are completed.

So, what is a leader? "Leader" is usually a label that we give to a person within an organization that has influence over our behaviour. They "lead" us to do certain things. Think of an influential person in your office, division, department, etc. How do they "lead" you?

It may not actually be the manager who influences you in this way. It may be a co-worker or someone who reports to you. Leaders are found at all levels within a company. Some may disagree with this statement. Some feel that leaders are only found at the top levels of an organization. If you believe this, you may overlook the tremendous impact that "leaders" have on other employees in the company — for good and for bad.

Leaders lead people to feel, think, act, and work in ways that they might not consider on their own.

Now, here's a question: "Who determines whether someone is a leader or not?" 1 would like to suggest that it is the "follower" who determines whether or not someone is a leader. So, if we consider someone a leader because of his influence on us, we have determined that the individual in question is a leader. If, for some reason, we do not wish to be influenced by an individual — even if it is someone who has been given a mandate to "lead" us, he is not a leader in our eyes and does not have the desired effect. Thus, leaders earn the right to lead.

What do good leaders do? I have asked this question of hundreds of executives in the years that I have been delivering leadership workshops and the lists are always the same:

- Made me feel inspired to do my best.
- Listened to me.
- Made me feel like I belong.
- Available to talk to when I need them.
- Made me feel like my work is valued.
- Involved me in decisions.
- Shared information with me.
- Provided feedback on my work.

- Honoured individual and group achievements.
- Listened to ideas and was open to innovation.

Very seldom did individuals or groups identify "technically knowledgeable" as one of the qualities or attributes of good leaders. This is an interesting observation. Often managers are chosen based on their superior technical ability. One engineer once told me, "the day they made me a manager, they lost an excellent engineer and gained a poor manager". He had no management skills and no management training and felt unprepared for the job.

In our groups we also make a list of what bad leaders do — which incidentally is the opposite of the "good leader list". So, how do we interpret this list? One of the questions I ask groups is, "how do good leaders learn to do these things?" Groups often struggle to answer this question. Ultimately, the answer is that learning to do the things good leaders do involves developing an additional set of competencies that provide a foundation upon which we can learn the skills listed.

For example, how do we inspire people to do their best? Well, first, we need to know and understand how we are inspired to do our best. Then we need to get inspired to do our best. Finally, we need to demonstrate those actions that communicate inspiration to others to do their best.

Let us consider how people are made to feel like they belong. First, we need to know and understand what makes us feel like we belong. Then we need to know and understand others to know what types of things make them feel like they belong. Finally, we need to behave in ways that communicate to individuals that they belong.

There is thus a trend in how we build this foundation of competencies. How do we know when we are "inspired" or if we "belong"? There is a whole lot to do with "feeling" and "emotions" here. What we need is to know more about feeling and emotions. What we need is to be "intelligent" about emotion. Let us consider what is known about "emotional intelligence".

WHAT IS EMOTIONAL INTELLIGENCE?

If you type "emotional intelligence" into your favourite Internet search engine, you will get approximately 1,180,000 websites containing the term "emotional intelligence". This begins what I sometimes call the "EQ Maze". There are so many different perspectives on emotional intelligence that it is difficult to tell which is the "correct" one. Rather than there being a "correct" perspective, let me tell you a little about what I consider to be important in determining which perspective is for you.

First, I think it is important that the definition makes sense to you as something that you can work with. If you are in Human Resources, then you need a definition and a theoretical perspective of emotional intelligence that can be measured and improved to assist you with your objective of developing more productive employees. While there may be more than one perspective that fits this bill, let me tell you about the perspective of Dr Rueven BarOn, a U.S.-educated Israeli who completed his Ph.D. studies in South Africa. Why Dr BarOn's perspective and not another? Dr BarOn's theory of emotional intelligence is one of the few that arise directly from empirical research and quantitative analysis of data.

Dr BarOn's work in the area began with his concern with why so many patients in his clinical psychology practice with high IQs seem to struggle with so many aspects of life. In other words, why do smart people do dumb things? Dr BarOn then set off to study what competencies differentiated people who did "smart" things, i.e., behaviours that assisted them to reach their stated objectives in life from people who did "dumb" things, i.e., behaviours which did not assist them to meet their own stated objectives.

His work was carried out in the context of creating an assessment tool to measure these "competencies". Dr BarOn's definition of emotional intelligence, what he initially called "social and emotional competence", is as follows:

> Emotional Intelligence is an array of noncognitive capabilities, competencies, and skills that influence one's ability to succeed in coping with environmental demands and pressures (Dr Rueven BarOn 1987).

If we think in terms of leadership skills, emotional intelligence then is the array of competencies that influence one's ability to succeed in coping with the demands and pressures of leading in a corporate environment.

Dr BarOn has described five general areas or "composite scales" of emotional intelligence competencies:

1. Intrapersonal
2. Interpersonal
3. Adaptability
4. Stress Management
5. General Mood

In the sections that follow, each composite scale will be introduced along with its subscales, including definitions.

I. Intrapersonal

Emotional Self-Awareness: The ability to recognize and understand one's feelings and emotions, differentiate between them, and know what caused them and why.

Benefit: In the workplace, good emotional self-awareness promotes successful conflict resolution and leads to improved interaction with staff. It allows one to "clear the air" by addressing issues directly and promptly without an avoidance that often makes things worse.

Assertiveness: The ability to express feelings, beliefs, and thoughts and defend one's fights in a constructive way.

Benefit: In the workplace, appropriate assertiveness helps individuals to work more cohesively and to share ideas effectively. Good leaders have well-developed assertiveness skills.

Self-Regard: The ability to look at and understand oneself, respect and accept oneself, accept one's perceived positive and negative aspects as well as one's limitations and possibilities.

Benefit: In the workplace, employees who have high self-regard have better work attitudes and behaviours. High self-regard often leads to better self-confidence, which, in turn, leads to higher performance.

Self-Actualization: The ability to realize one's potential capacities and to strive to do that which one wants to do and enjoys doing.

Benefit: In the workplace, high self-actualization is connected with good motivation and with the ability to optimize both individual and team performance. A well-rounded individual brings more life experience to the job.

Independence: The ability to be self-reliant and self-directed in one's thinking and actions and to be free of emotional dependency; these people may ask for and consider the advice of others, but they rarely depend on others to make important decisions or do things for them.

Benefit: In the workplace, the proper balance is for leaders to ultimately "think for themselves" and yet still listen to and incorporate ideas from others when appropriate.

II. Interpersonal

Interpersonal Relationship: The ability to establish and maintain mutually satisfying relationships that are characterized by intimacy and by giving and receiving affection.

Benefit: In the workplace, good interpersonal relations translate into effective communication within and between individuals, teams, departments, and divisions.

Empathy: The ability to be attentive to, to understand, and to appreciate the feelings of others; it is being able to "emotionally read" other people.

Benefit: In the workplace, understanding the impact of the duties and demands being placed on staff members creates cohesive functioning. Understanding others' points of view will help in leading others more effectively.

Social Responsibility: The ability to demonstrate oneself as a cooperative, contributing, and constructive member of one's social group.

Benefit: In the workplace, social responsibility means contributing to recognized departmental and company goals. A good leader is also a team player. It also means being aware of the greater good the individual and his group can contribute to society as a whole.

III. Adaptability

Problem Solving: The ability to identify and define problems as well as to generate and implement potentially effective solutions.

Benefit: In the workplace, the method used for problem solving is critical — viable alternative solutions must be considered, including a cost/benefit analysis and long-term implications.

Reality Testing: The ability to assess the correspondence between what is experienced (the subjective) and what exists in reality (the objective).

Benefit: In the workplace, the focus should be on practicality and not unrealistic expectations.

Flexibility: The ability to adjust one's emotions, thoughts, and behaviour to changing situations and conditions.

Benefits: In the workplace, those high in flexibility perform better in positions where tasks are dynamic and changing. Those low in flexibility may perform better at more well-defined tasks requiring reliability and consistency.

IV. Stress Management

Stress Tolerance: The ability to withstand adverse events and stressful situations without falling apart by actively and confidently coping with stress.

Benefit: In the workplace, effective stress tolerance has to do with managing reasonable workloads, establishing clear priorities, and meeting realistic deadlines.

Impulse Control: The ability to resist or delay an impulse, drive, or temptation to act.

Benefit: In the workplace, rash actions can be costly. Mistakes can often be avoided by simply taking time to stop and think.

V. General Mood

Happiness: The ability to feel satisfied with one's life, to enjoy oneself and being with others, and to have fun.

Benefit: In the workplace, a positive atmosphere lifts spirits and helps overall performance.

Optimism: The ability to look at the brighter side of life and to maintain a positive attitude, even in the face of adversity.

Benefit: In the workplace, there is such a thing as a self-fulfilling prophecy. When employees believe something is possible, they will often make it happen. An optimistic attitude also helps ward off stress.

DEVELOPING EMOTIONAL INTELLIGENCE

How can leaders develop their emotional intelligence? Let's first look at how we as human beings develop our emotional intelligence. It begins in infancy when our significant caregivers "teach" us to be comforted and to comfort ourselves, and later on, to comfort others. In psychological literature, this self-comfort is called "self-soothing". This is the beginning of emotional self-awareness. Then, for example, as toddlers we learn from significant others that we must control some of our basic drives and temptations and we learn impulse control. We get all kinds of messages from our caregivers as we grow and we incorporate those into our self-regard, independence, etc. All of our experiences contribute to our developing emotional intelligence.

The most interesting thing about this process is that it is not systematic, nor is it fully intentional, or consistent, therefore, some people have excellent teachers and learn their lessons well and others do not.

One of the leading organizations in the world for the development of emotional intelligence is the Six Seconds EQ Network in San Francisco, CA. The introduction to one of their publications notes that aliens from another planet would be very intrigued upon studying our societies down here on earth to find that we have a systematic, fully intentional, and consistent system for the development of IQ, but we leave EQ or the development of emotional intelligence totally to chance.

So, how do we as adults develop our emotional intelligence? Well, the best way I know of is to work one-to-one with someone in a coaching or counselling relationship. After coaching or counselling, group courses and workshops are the next best way to develop emotional intelligence, and following that, there are a lot of resources available for those who want to learn more on their own. In each case, the steps involved are to learn more about your current level of emotional intelligence through the use of an assessment tool. One of the best on the market is Dr Rueven BarOn's Emotional Quotient Inventory (EQ-i), which is a 133-item, web-enabled, scientifically-validated assessment or inventory of one's emotional intelligence competencies. Also available is the EQ-360, which is based on the EQ-i and is based on the same model of emotional intelligence.

CONCLUSION

Leaders create the context within which we work. Leaders can create a productive, happy, healthy context where employees feel valued, inspired, motivated, and where they feel they can produce their best work. Likewise, leaders can create the opposite environment where employees feel dread as they think about entering the work environment and, given the choice, they would leave the organization at the first opportunity. Given the importance of leaders and leadership on the effectiveness and, hence, on the productivity of an organization, leaders must, therefore, understand how to inspire and ignite passion to make employees happy and keep employees healthy, so they stay and contribute to their full potential for their whole careers.

REFERENCES

BarOn, R. "Emotional and Social Intelligence: Insights from the Emotional Quotient Inventory (EQ-i)". In R. BarOn and J.D.A. Parker (eds.), *Handbook of Emotional Intelligence*. San Francisco: JosseyBass, 2000.

BarOn, R. and R. Handley. *Optimizing People: A practical guide for applying emotional intelligence to improve personal and organizational effectiveness.* New Braunfels: TX Pro-Philes Press, 1999.

Goleman, Daniel. *Emotional Intelligence: Why It Can Matter More Than IQ*. New York: Bantam Books, 1995.

Goleman, Daniel. *Working With Emotional Intelligence*. New York: Bantam Books, 1998.

Goleman, Daniel. *Primal Leadership*. New York: Bantam Books, 2001.

Stein, Steven and Howard Book. *The EQ Edge: Emotional Intelligence and Your Success*. Toronto, Ontario: MHS, Inc, 1999.

Websites of Interest

www.eiconsortium.org — leaders in the field of Emotional Intelligence.

www.mhs.com — MHS publishes the assessment for EI (Emotional Quotient Inventory — EQ-I and the EQ-360) and has a lot of information and research papers available on their site.

www.6seconds.org — leaders in the development of EI curricula for children and adults.

www.eqi.org — the EQ Institute — review of all literature pertaining to EI.

www.davidcory.com — for information on assessing emotional intelligence using the EQ-i or EQ-360 and for information about becoming certified to use the EQ-i and the EQ-360, also for information on workshops and seminars custom designed to address the unique needs of your organization.

11

Diversity in Work-Life Programmes

Gerardo A. Plana

Managing diversity is one of the greatest challenges of the twenty-first century. The ability to understand and harmonize differences and achieve shared goals is one of the most valuable competencies required of effective people managers. The concept of treating everyone equally is now being replaced by the emphasis on individualism. Gone are the days of "one size fits all". Understanding diversity in work-life issues becomes particularly important as a growing number of people clamour for a more "balanced life" as a precondition for sustained performance. A balanced life varies from person to person depending on personal circumstances. In short, work-life balance means different things to different people. Work-life balance solutions must recognize the unique needs of people. A simple way of defining work-life balance is to refer to a satisfying and productive life that includes work, play, and love. There are many facets of life: economic, social, physical, mental, and spiritual. Work-life balance is not necessarily about giving equal amounts of time to all aspects of life. Balance is a key principle in life. Getting out of balance can get someone into serious trouble. Oftentimes, we are confronted with a situation where work and life conflict. This is usually defined as the tension that arises when work and personal life compete with each other in which a gain in one area means a loss in the other.

There is a strong business case for linking balance with productivity. This link should encourage organizations to promote work-life balance among employees. Diagnosing an organization's work-life balance requirements requires looking into certain principles and the extent they are practised in organizations. These include the following:

- **Culture** — The culture of the organization creates an environment in which work-life balance is recognized and valued.

- **Strategy** — The work-life balance strategy is central to the organization's aims and objectives.
- **Action** — The organization has successful work-life balance solutions.
- **Effectiveness** — The organization can show that its work-life balance strategy is delivering positive results.

Once the diagnosis is completed, the appropriate work-life balance programmes are implemented and monitored. These programmes include flexitime, job sharing, telecommuting, child/elder care services, company gatherings that include families, and so on. Evaluation measures include attraction and retention of talent, health costs, productivity, and absenteeism.

Preparing an organization to undertake these initiatives requires the development of the necessary competencies on the subject. Different types of people will require different types of competency preparation. For instance, the senior management team would need, first of all, to challenge some of their most cherished assumptions that are anti-balance. Once this is accomplished, these executives can be taught to develop strategies and policies that promote work-life balance. The HR team needs to be proficient in diagnosing work-life issues and recommending and implementing the appropriate work-life balance programmes. Line managers should have the basic skill of identifying work-life issues and doing some counselling work. Finally, employees need to be helped in analyzing their priorities in life and developing a work-life balance plan.

The challenge of addressing diversity in work-life issues can no longer be postponed. Organizations must squarely face the reality that if they do not go for balance, they will be greatly handicapped in an age where everyone is constantly competing for the best talent in the market.

12

Strategic HR — Making Do or Doing More?

Anthony O'Hara

My focus is on the use and role of information technology in meeting the challenges facing Human Resources (HR). The functions of HR have expanded tremendously over the years in such a way that very few organizations are now able to perform these diverse roles effectively. The core functions of HR can be summarized thus:

Labour Sourcing
- Demand forecasting
- Recruiting
- Contractor Hiring
- Supplier Relations
- Offer Negotiations
- On-Boarding

Workforce Management
- People-Deployment
- Development
- Compensation

Services Labour Relations
- Compliance
- Organizations

Post-Employment
- Termination
- Benefits
- Re-Hires

- References
- Records

In the face of contemporary business realities, some questions elucidating the pressures and considerations that HR must be faced:

Development and Retention
- How can I develop an agile workforce to support my changing business?
- How can I attract workers with key competencies and skills?

Global Dispersion
- What is the best way to service an increasingly global, multi-cultural workforce?
- How can I keep pace with changing safety regulations and privacy laws?

Motivation
- Which jobs and assignments are most rewarding and interesting?
- What are the competitive strengths and weaknesses of our compensation plans?

Cost Control
- Where can I cut costs and improve workforce management efficiencies?
- How can I manage and improve workforce utilization?

Thus, HR needs to move up the chain not only to provide better value services to the employees but also better value information to the management. Solutions adopted by HR to carry out these diverse roles efficiently must be capable of providing an end-to-end view of HR, linking business visions with outcomes. This requires the integration of the complex plethora of HR information to allow for business questions to be readily answered. The use of information technology (IT) is key to these solutions. Thus it would be naïve to think that HR is well positioned to carry out these more complex roles simply through a sole reliance on sheer will power, culture and personnel. Technology has indeed altered the playing field, impacting upon budgets and the competitive advantage of a business, a corporation, an organization or even a country.

Overall, there has been an increasing awareness of the "Cost of Human Capital". As the workforce is the biggest expense of any corporation, business or even governments, it is very important that measures are developed to quantify performance and productivity. Research has also shown that knowledge workers spend a lot of time dealing with content and creating documents. As such, it is equally important to install tools that allow for a more effective content management in order to enable these workers do their job well.

The fragmentation of HR data is the single biggest operational challenge. Data fragmentation is an inevitable aspect of how governments and multinational companies operate today. Technological tools are already available to help corporations and governments overcome the inefficiencies that can arise as a result of this. However, the most important thing is to be able to want to change and to adopt these tools. Architectural limitations can affect HR contributions as well, leading to fragmented customer data, manual processes and information silos. Given these realities, it is crucial for HR to move away from its traditional skew of services, which includes ad hoc, low value and transactional requests, and focus instead on delivering more in terms of organizational benefit by driving value to the business, and linking strategies with outcomes. Today this can be achieved through integrating information technology in HR management processes. Nevertheless, IT solutions adopted to carry out these higher value-added HR management processes should have the following key capabilities:

- Extensive online capabilities for recruiters, managers and applicants to optimally source the workforce.
- Rapid restructuring tools, objectives-based career development and learning management, performance-based total competition to align workforce to organizational benefits.
- Role-based portal access and productivity tools and integrated partner content to connect people, content and community.
- Single global instance with multi-national/-lingual capabilities and compliance and daily business intelligence to compete globally and focus locally.
- Workflow-driven automation and self-service applications and financial integration to decrease costs while increasing value.

COMPETENCE
DEVELOPMENT

13

Creating Sustainable Competitive Advantage Through People and Culture

Günter Stahl

The objective of this paper is to provide a broad overview of current trends in HRM and leadership development, and to give participants an idea how some of the most successful companies manage their people and culture.

What we can observe today in the most successful companies is a clear trend away from HRM as a mere cost function to driver of firm performance and sustainable competitive advantage. This trend goes hand in hand with a belief in the efficiency of so called **"high performance" work systems** or **HRM practices**. There is strong research evidence to suggest that high-performing companies adopt HRM practices different from those adopted by low-performing firms (e.g., study of U.S. companies conducted by Mark Huselid and colleagues such as *The Workforce Scorecard: Managing Human Capital to Execute Strategy* [Harvard Business School Press, 2005]).

Based on this and related research, Jeff Pfeffer concluded that seven **HRM practices** are particularly effective in improving firm performance.

1) *Highly selective hiring*: e.g., Southwest Airlines in 1993 received 98,000 applications, interviewed 16,000 people, and eventually hired 2,700. Infosys last year (in 2004), despite the increasing competition for software engineers in India, received over one million applications, they tested around 130,000 candidates, and hired 10,000 — the top 1%, based on their assessment results. Companies can only be highly selective in hiring when they have a large applicant pool. And, these companies need efficient and validated selection processes. Also, Pfeffer found that some of the most successful companies focus on attitudes and cultural fit, rather than job-related skills, in the selection process. Kelleher, the former CEO of SWA, puts it this way: "If you don't have

a good attitude, we don't want you, no matter how skilled you are. We can change skill levels through training; we can't change attitudes".

2) *Extensive training*: Emphasis on training is a logical consequence of the fact that these companies focus on attitudes and cultural fit, rather than job-related skills, in the selection process.

3) *Self-managed teams*: Team-based organizations are more successful in having all of the employees feel accountable and responsible for the success of the firm. Teams also permit employees to pool their ideas to come up with better and more creative solutions to problems.

4) *Reduction of status differences*: Some of the most successful companies have reduced the gross wage differences between top managers and the rest of the employees. Some companies have practised this philosophy from day one. At SWA, for example, there are no company cars, no club memberships, and Herb Kelleher, former CEO of Southwest, was one of the lowest paid CEOs in the United States.

5) *Employment security*: Employment security is fundamental to implementation of most of the other high performance HRM practices, e.g., investment in training and development. Also, Pfeffer found that companies tend to lay off people too quickly at the first sign of financial difficulty.

6) *Compensation contingent on performance*: Employee stock ownership is an important part of the compensation and benefits systems of many of the most successful companies. The philosophy behind employee stock ownership plans is that "When employees are owners, they think and act like owners". Unfortunately, there is little evidence that stock ownership, by itself, affects individual or firm performance. In order to be effective, stock ownership programmes have to be part of a broader philosophy of management that incorporates other practices, such as training and development, information sharing, and delegation of responsibility.

7) *Information sharing*: Most of the top-performing companies have developed and implemented comprehensive measurement systems such as the Balanced Scorecard (BSC) for communicating financial and non-financial information to employees. In addition to the direct positive effect of enhanced communication, information sharing on such things as financial performance, strategy, etc., conveys to employees that they are trusted by management and thus has a motivational effect.

As an integrated system, not in isolation, these practices have a powerful impact on the performance of companies. At least, this is what studies of North-American companies have found, and there is also some evidence from outside the United States, mainly from Europe.

But there are caveats.

Contrary to what HRM scholars such as Pfeffer and Huselid propose, HRM practices — management practices in general — are not universally effective; their effectiveness depends on **cultural fit**. For example, pay for performance systems, reduction of status differences or extensive delegation of control may not work as well in some Asian countries.

Also, what might be more important than adopting the specific HRM practices suggested by Peffer, is that the various elements of a company's HRM system fit together. **Internal alignment** is crucial. To be effective, HRM practices must be internally consistent, complementary and reinforcing — they must be part of an integrated system. Implementing practices in isolation may not have much effect or may even be counter-productive. For example, increasing the firm's commitment to training and development will not have much impact on firm performance unless changes in job design and work organization allow employees to use their newly acquired knowledge and skills at work. Or, if wages are relatively low and incentives are lacking, the best-trained people may leave the organization to join a competitor.

Furthermore, HRM practices must be closely **linked to the business strategy** and help the company achieve key business goals such as better customer service, enhanced productivity, innovation, etc. — strategic fit is critical. More and more companies are using the "**Balanced Scorecard**" to align HRM practices with the business strategy.

HRM in the most successful companies is closely associated with **values-based leadership and cultural control**. Successful companies often have systems of HR practices that are embodied in some philosophy of management or value system that provides meaning and coherence. For example, many of the leading companies (e.g., IBM and HP, CitiBank and HSBC, J&J and Novartis) are now starting to reward managers for dis-playing shared values — for behaviour that is consistent with the core values of the organization — rather than for meeting short-term performance targets. For example, Novartis has implemented a new Performance Management System that combines two dimensions: the achievement of the performance objectives (WHAT) and the related values and behaviours required to deliver the results (HOW). So Novartis managers are assessed on not only how well they perform but also on shared values and related behaviours in their annual performance appraisal.

And, finally, there is strong evidence to suggest that HRM today is closely associated with the **management of change** and **organizational learning** and **knowledge management**.

To conclude, there is a clear trend away from HRM as a mere cost function that is responsible mainly for administrative tasks, toward HRM as driver of firm performance and sustainable competitive advantage; HR professionals, in these companies, are recognized as change agents and strategic partners.

14

Maximizing Workforce Efficiencies with Effective Change Management

Victor S.L. Tan

A survey conducted by the Conference Board in 2000, which polled 5,000 U.S. companies shows that less than half of all workers in different age groups and income levels are satisfied with their work. According to Towers Perrin HR Services in an article published in 2004, employees in a number of European countries share one disturbing trend — deepening dissatisfaction with their work experience and disenchantment with their company's management. Likewise, having worked with over 300 Asian organizations, I have experienced a trend of growing dissatisfaction among the workers and a decline in workforce productivity. To improve workforce productivity, I recommend that corporate leaders address the three critical challenges facing organizations today:

1. Change the mindsets of the workforce as well as the leaders themselves;
2. Eliminate the sense of complacency in the workplace, and;
3. Address the issue of unproductive competency in people. I propose that leaders do this through developing and utilizing change management skills.

WHAT IS CHANGE MANAGEMENT?

Change management is the process of initiating changes within an organization aligned to the external environment to enable it to stay relevant, efficient and competitive.

The core of change management is changing the mindsets of people to get them to accept or initiate changes to enable the organization to achieve its goals effectively and efficiently

Defining Mindset: Mindset is the state of mind that is influenced by the beliefs of person, which in turn determine the thinking, feeling and action towards a certain situation that requires change.

Strategy I: Changing the Mindset of the Workforce

To improve workforce efficiency and productivity, leaders need to get people to change their mindsets in response to changes around them, be it a new system, process, technology, strategy or a new way of working altogether.

The greatest challenge in organizations today is changing the mindsets of its people. Too many are struggling to change but remain more the same as each year goes by. The reality is that an organization can only change if the mindsets of the people change. Changing the system, process, technology, structure and strategy is not enough.

How then do you get people to change their mindset? I recommend the following:

Getting people to see the need for change

One of the least effective ways to get people to change is to tell them to do so. Yet many leaders simply tell their people to change. They do this in their speeches, through memos, e-mails, posters and meetings. Of course the results are frustrating. After a while, these leaders get so desperate that they start shouting and forcing people to change. Of course such efforts are counter-productive, since they will create more resistance towards change. The first important step is to get people see the need for change. The idea is to get people see the reasons for change for themselves. For example, you cannot simply force someone to wear glasses. But if we can prove to a person that he or she has early signs of shortsightedness and if he or she knows that wearing glasses will provide her with better vision and prevent further deterioration, he or she might be persuaded to change.

Communicate a powerful rationale of change

Getting people to see the need for change is only a first small step. Often, to get people to go beyond the need for change, they must be gripped by a powerful rationale for change. For example, getting people to work hard to reach a target is not a strong enough rationale. But getting people to improve their productivity to prevent the parent company from closing the production outlet in Malaysia and moving it to China is a powerful rationale. This change suddenly becomes gripping because it is not just increasing productivity for the company, it is now about keeping jobs and maintaining livelihoods.

Getting people out of their comfort zone

People will not change as long as they are in their comfort zone. Human beings are driven by pain and pleasure. As long as it remains more comfortable not to change than change, one will continue with the status quo. For example in my seminars, I have asked participants which they preferred: To stand up or sit down throughout the two-day programmes. All indicated they preferred sitting. When I asked them why, they responded that it was more comfortable sitting than standing. However, when I said that if I were to put thumbtacks on the chair, which would they then prefer. All indicated they would then prefer standing, the reason being that in this case it would be more painful to sit than to stand. Likewise, to get people out of their comfort zone, we need to create a sense of urgency and in particular the threat of pain if they stay where they are. For example, to get people to perform, do not pay bonuses across the board. Deprive those who do not perform of bonuses or other benefits. That should be made to get them out of their comfort zone.

Getting people to unlearn old ways

Before one can learn a new way, one has to unlearn the old, especially if the latter is preventing one from changing. Just like in the game of baseball, you cannot get to second base by hanging on to first base. Yes, moving from first base to second base involves risk; you might be struck out of the game. Likewise, letting go of old ways and adopting a new approach involves risk. While it is not possible to eliminate risk altogether, one can make it safer for people to change. This can be done through training, coaching and providing the needed support to succeed with the new way.

Getting people to view change positively

Change is difficult if one views it from a negative standpoint. Attitude will determine whether change is accepted or not. Without acceptance, the individuals will not make any effort to change. Getting the right person to deliver the right message across in the right manner is critical. Too often, a change being introduced, though inherently positive, is communicated in a way that elicits a negative attitude in others. Perhaps it is the lack of openness and transparency in the way it is communicated. Sometimes, it is the fault of the person who delivers the message. When there is no trust in the leader, whatever changes recommended by him or her will be rejected. Thus to make it work, it is important to elicit a positive attitude towards change by taking the right approach with the right message through the right leader.

Strategy II: Eliminating the Sense of Complacency

The greatest threat facing an organization today is not the competition. Neither is it the increasing demands placed by customers. Nor is the pace of change brought about by globalization. The greatest threat to the survival of organizations today is the complacency of people within. This is the number one enemy in large and successful organizations today. When an organization is small and thriving, leaders are up and about addressing customer service issues, quality problems and productivity challenges. They are committed to doing everything to stay competitive and win market share and get the company to grow. However, as the company starts to grow in leaps and bounds and achieve considerable success, people begin to get too comfortable for their own good. They begin to lull into complacency in every area of work where they once placed great importance in. It is this sense of complacency that leads to the fall of an organization.

Complacency in the workplace is defined here as a sense of excessive comfort coupled with a lack of urgency to address organization issues or areas that need improvement and growth.

There are six grave dangers of complacency:

1. Complacency leads to blind spots
One of the greatest dangers of complacency is that it creates blind spots in people towards the need for change and growth. Blind spots refer to those critical areas that need to be addressed but are not since people are not aware of them or refuse to acknowledge them. In fact, prior to the Asian Financial Crisis, due to a string of successes achieved by organizations, many leaders began to develop blind spots towards the need for better risk management. They began to expose their companies to excessive risks to the extent that one failed investment or venture could bring the whole organization down. Leaders in successful companies develop blind spots in many areas because of their refusal to see changes around them and the impact these have on their companies. The strings of achievements and successes they have achieved have blinded them to potential dangers. Often success brings out the sense of arrogance and overconfidence in

leaders. These elements cloud their thinking and block their understanding of the actual issues. Blind spots develop because leaders are blinded by past successes and thus have the vision of their future blocked.

2. Complacency lowers quality

In a booming business environment where demand exceeds supply, it is easy for people in organizations to take the business for granted. In the rush to fulfil orders, the trade-off is quality for quantity, justified by the rationale that quality does not count much when there are lots of customers. Many take the attitude that in view of the good business, even if the company is to lose some customers, it does not matter because there are still other customers around. It is this sense of complacency that leads to poor quality products and service. In a booming business environment, this strategic flaw is camouflaged by new customers. However, these new customers are also soon lost. The impact of poor quality is often not discerned until it is too late, and has long-term and strategic implications. Customers who are not happy with a company's products or services will not only stop doing business with it but will inform ten other people they know about their dissatisfaction. The tarnished image from poor quality products or services will undo millions and often billions of dollars of goodwill gained from advertisement and branding. It will cost five times more to get a new customer than to retain an existing customer. Customers who are not happy with the quality of products or services of a company give the business to its competitors.

3. Complacency leads to excess

One of the great ills that come from complacency is the tendency towards excess. Companies who are doing well become lax in their control of resources. Departments and divisions become overstaffed, thus incurring unnecessary resources. Overtime and expenses of staff claims shoot up. Companies acquire a lot of unnecessary and unproductive assets such as excessive office renovations and décor. Granted that company image is important, but going overboard with a luxurious head office, generous perks for top executives such as huge executive rooms expensively furnished, expensive cars, big expense allowances and unjustifiably fat bonuses will certainly increase the overall cost of the organization. This excess necessarily affects the productivity and competitiveness of the company. If an increase in cost is due to increased investment, advertisement and the employment of additional staff to cope with increasing workload, then that is fine. Cost increases that have no direct or indirect impact on increasing business have to be curtailed as much as possible. Recurring costs such as huge increments to reward higher performance that are not sustainable will only lead to excesses. To prevent excesses, it may be wise to provide one-time non-recurring incentives to staff who have help achieved certain target figures.

4. Complacency leads to inaction and maintains the status quo

Success results from the taking of necessary actions. In fact, one of the hallmarks of successful companies is that they act a lot. They undertake customer satisfaction surveys and take quick action to address customer complaints. They undertake market research and continuously improve products and services to meet the changing needs of customers. They innovate to fend off competition and increase their market share. Leaders listen to staff and address their needs to enable them to stay productive. They plan, train and develop staff to increase the overall competency level of the organization. They take great effort in motivating and rewarding people based on performance. However, success breeds complacency, and that eventually leads to inaction. There are many stories of successful companies that eventually fall because people in organizations stop taking necessary action. The downfall begins when they stop improving, changing and expanding the organizations. Many leaders and staff in successful companies reach a point where they feel they no longer need to act. They rest on their laurels. Instead of making things happen, they are immobilized by the status quo. They become passive and wait for things to happen. They hope that the momentum created by the success will move things forward on their own. The truth is that things do not move on their own unless someone moves them.

5. Complacency leads to strategic vulnerabilities

One of the greatest dangers of complacency is the building up of strategic vulnerabilities. Strategic vulnerabilities refer to the weaknesses or flaws that expose the company to risks. Thus a company that does not undertake market surveys to understand changing customer needs may continue producing what customers no longer need. This is a strategic flaw that in time will lead to collapse. Likewise, a company that has poor cash management may find itself not capable of paying debtors, and become insolvent. This can lead to the demise of the company altogether. Such complacency is tantamount to a person cutting his own wrist, and unless the bleeding is stopped, death is the certain outcome. When leaders are complacent, they no longer think strategically about the future of the company. They become too comfortable with their past and current successes. Their thinking becomes excessively short-term, inward looking and narrow. They no longer assess the threats facing the organization. By not taking action or addressing strategic issues fast enough, they expose the company to grave dangers. Thus, not addressing the entrance of a new competitor into the industry and not countering threats posed by new products may create strategic vulnerabilities in the company. Complacency leads to the underestimation of threats.

6. Complacency leads to deterioration of bottom line performance

Complacency affects the bottom line performance of a company in many ways, both in the short- and long-term. Being complacent, people may not explore new products, new services or new markets. Missed opportunities affect the potential revenue growth of the company. Complacent organizations that no longer put emphasis on quality problems and customer complaints will lose customers and sales revenue. Complacent organizations tend to have operation staff that chalk up production costs, and support staff that balloon head office expenditures. This increases overall costs and squeezes the profit margin. In a very competitive and fast changing environment, maintaining the status quo is the surest path to losing market share. Organizations that become complacent and do not change or expand fast will see their profits evaporate quickly. Complacency thus brings a host of undesirable behaviour that leads to a deteriorating bottom line performance that eventually decimates the whole organization.

To eliminate complacency, organizations need to take action to reduce comfort and build a sense of urgency. There are six strategies that organizations can adopt to rid themselves of complacency:

a) **Practise Strong Leadership** — One of the root causes of complacency is weak leadership. Weak leaders shun their role of enforcing discipline. They strive to be popular to the detriment of the organization. They are afraid to point out poor performance or non-compliance. They tend to tolerate non-punctuality, the lack of cleanliness, missed deadlines, poor quality, poor performance or non-performance. They continue to harp on the importance of these matters but take little action to back up their words. They cannot make firm decisions about change. They often hesitate and waver when fast action is needed. They are subject to the pressure of resistance and often reverse decisions when faced with objections from the staff. Weak leadership allows complacency to foster and spread.

Effective leadership is strong leadership. To eliminate complacency, leaders must take the necessary action to address issues in a very decisive and persistent manner. They need to stick out their neck for staff that perform, and fight for their recognition. Likewise, they need to make unpopular decisions to penalize chronic non-performers. If it is needed, they may have to fire those who continue with their non-performance in order to send a strong message throughout the organization. Likewise, disciplinary action should be taken in the strictest manner. Only through the practice of strong leadership can complacency be eliminated or reduced.

b) **Adopt Transparent SMART Goals** — Complacency is prevalent in organizations that lack a transparent way of measuring and communicating performance. An effective way is first to set clear and measurable performance goals for a department or unit. Each unit must set SMART goals (Specific, Measurable, Actionable, Realistic, Time-driven). For example, a research and development unit may set up a goal of developing three new and innovative products and have them market-tested by the end of the year. The individuals in this department will then be asked to set SMART individual goals to help achieve this goal. All the SMART goals in this research and development unit should add up and result in the achievement of the department's goal.

To reduce complacency, it will be good to get each department to communicate their SMART goals to other departments. Likewise, individual SMART goals should also be openly communicated to others. Getting individuals to declare their SMART goals to others will not only further reinforce their commitment but also create the pressure and sense of urgency needed for achieving them. Personal pride and integrity are at stake since the individual's pledges and duties suddenly become measurable and visible to others. This should be followed by open communication about the achievement of the results. When results are transparent, it is difficult for anyone to be complacent.

c) **Hold People Accountable for Results** — The truth is, no matter how little has been said, talk is still a promise. Specific action is an instalment towards the promise. Positive result is the actual delivery, the promise made good. To help reduce complacency in the workplace, hold people accountable for results. Thus departments or units are held accountable for their SMART goals. Likewise department heads or leaders must hold individuals responsible for achieving their respective SMART goals. To reduce complacency, leaders must move people from promise to action and from action to the desired results, get people to stay focused on achieving results, and get people away from "blamestorming" about why they fail to achieve accountable results. One should instead get them to brainstorm on how they can help one another achieve the SMART goals of the department as well as their own individual goals and desired results. When people do not achieve their goals, the following series of questions should arise:

- What are the reasons for the goals not being achieved?
- Knowing the actual reasons, what can be done differently now to achieve the goals?
- What are the specific activities and the timeline for achieving the goals?
- When can a report on the progress status be made?

d) **Follow Up On Results And Corrective Actions** — In my Changing Mindset seminar, I often asked the audience to see himself or herself as a sprint coach. My question to them is: "How do you get your sprinter to run very fast?" I pointed out that a normal sprint coach equips his athletes well with branded spike shoes, a powerful starting block and comes to the field with a firing gun and a digital timer. After all the training provided, when it is time to run, the normal instruction a coach provides is: "When I fire the gun, I want you to run as fast as you can. In other words do your best". The problem with this approach is that complacency sets in and the effort of "doing your best" comes to merely trying. The way to reduce complacency that I propose is to bring along a tiger in a cage each time the coach gets the sprinter to run. The instruction should therefore be: "When I fire this gun, I will release the tiger from the cage and it will chase you from behind. I want you to run very fast". When the tiger is chasing from behind, complacency automatically disappears and one cannot afford to just try to do your best. The athlete definitely has to outrun the tiger to stay alive! To eliminate complacency we need people to get that same sense of urgency. After all, living in the corporate world with keen competition all around is a real case of "running faster ahead of your competitors to stay alive".

Of course the story I relate above is symbolic. Releasing a tiger from the cage is tantamount to first setting higher targets (in the case of the athlete, a faster time and for an individual, a higher target). The story also symbolizes the need to follow up with expected results or desired corrective actions — in the case of the athlete, to run faster to stay alive and for the corporate world to do better than the competitors to stay in business. The moral of the story is that to achieve success, do not just do whatever you can, you must do whatever it takes. It is only through constant follow-up and corrective actions that results are achieved. In fact, the most effective way to get people to be less complacent is to benchmark against the best and set higher goals.

e)   **Benchmark Against the Best** — An effective way to wipe out the sense of superiority after an organization has won many awards and achieved quantum leap improvements is to continue to benchmark against the best. If a company is number two, it should benchmark against the number one in the industry. If it is already number one in the industry locally, it should benchmark against the very top in the world. The way to eliminate the sense of complacency arising from great achievements is to continue to set higher and higher goals and build a larger dream and vision for the organization as well as for the employees. The role of leaders is to provide industry information and competitors' increasing achievements in order to decrease the level of complacency within the organization. Information such as threats in the industry with increasingly competitive pricing, increasing customer sophistication, potential entry of new competitors, and substitutes of the company products should be communicated to the staff to help eliminate the sense of complacency. A director of operations at one of our seminars started with a very strong opening statement to the participants: "If as a company we do not find ways to be innovative and productive, we will not be able to compete with the lower cost production of competitors in China. And if we cannot compete with China, I am afraid this company may cease its local production soon and relocate to China". While such a statement may sound like a threat, it is very real. It is also an effective wake-up call for the staff to buck up and continue to be better. It is truly a corporate jungle out there, and the theory about the survival of the fittest theory is still very relevant.

f) **Eliminate Corporate Politics** — One of the greatest dampers to productivity in organizations is company politics. In company politics, the staff often plays to the tune of the leaders to get away with work. Many non-performers talk up instead of work up the corporate ladder. When performers in organizations see that hard work and results do not matter, they will not take performance seriously. Companies that encourage corporate politics are providing an escape route for non-performers. This will breed a sense of complacency towards performance not only with non-performers but also with existing performers. Thus, to eliminate complacency towards performance, leaders must discourage corporate politics. They should make it clear that promotions and rewards in an organization are very much based on performance. The clearer the leaders set their performance measures and the more transparent they make the achievement results of people, the lesser room there is for corporate politics to loom. Instead of entertaining the common political manoeuvres of individuals, leaders should persist and insist that the decision to favour one or the other is purely based on clearly set criteria of performance. No amount of currying of favour will bring out the spice of reward except merit.

Strategy III: Addressing Unproductive Competences in People

Companies waste millions of dollars each year training their employees. And more millions are wasted in recruiting very qualified and experienced staff without ever utilizing the actual talents of these people. Our findings from 200 Asian organizations indicate that up to 75% of these companies experience this phenomenon called "unproductive competency". What is unproductive competency? Unproductive competency is the wasted skill, knowledge, experience or training that are not utilized in the workplace, due to many factors that block performance.

To address this very significant issue of unproductive competency, it is important that leaders first understand what the possible causes that create this phenomenon in organizations are. The following are the seven reasons why organizations suffer from unproductive competency.

1) **People are not provided the opportunity** — One of the most common causes for unproductive competency is that people are not given the opportunity to put what they know into practice. This is like some

American Football coaches who keep talented footballers sitting on the bench without giving them a chance to play a game. In the corporate world, there are also many talented corporate people who are sitting pretty in their executive chairs since their superiors do not allow them to undertake the challenging tasks. Of course, there are many underlying reasons why this is the case. Some leaders are insecure people and they may fear that their able subordinates may prove their mettle in a conspicuous manner if given the opportunity. Others simply have poor delegation skills and hog the key task and thus deprive their talented staff of the chance of utilizing their skills and experience to the fullest. Of course, there are leaders who fail to realize the talent of others. And then there are leaders who do not trust their people to do the work right. When people are deprived of using their talents, skills and knowledge, the competencies of these people are trapped and therefore are unproductive.

2) **People are not motivated to apply what they know** — Leaders often pride themselves in having sent their staff for training to upgrade their skills and knowledge. Some organizations pay millions of dollars sending their top executives overseas to attend conferences and seminars. However, few organizations really assess the degree to which these participants apply their knowledge in the workplace. There is a gap between knowing and actually doing it. It is like the difference between knowing all the mechanics of what it takes to lose weight and actually practising those good eating habits to shed the pounds. The gap is in the motivation and discipline. Organizations often develop unproductive competencies because trained staff sees no motivation in applying what they know in the workplace. It is not uncommon in organizations that people who are up and about, doing more things and trying new ways of doing things and achieving positive results are viewed no differently from the others. If leaders do not recognize people for their achievements, the motivation of people to apply what they know will be low. To apply new knowledge and skills in the workplace requires discipline, which in turn needs the right motivation to bring about. Without motivation, knowledge and skills will not be put to productive use.

3) **Superiors override subordinates' better ideas** — Sad to say, some organizations have great ideas and yet they implement the lesser ideas. The reason is because many superiors override the better ideas of their

subordinates. It does not make sense to hire someone with experience and talent and not tap his or her new ideas. Likewise, it is illogical when staff that are sent for training have their suggestions or new ideas vetoed by their bosses. Leaders who override the better ideas of people are making the phenomenon of unproductive competency prevalent in their organizations. The value of an organization lies not in the great knowledge of the people but in the application of this knowledge to achieve better results.

4) **People are afraid to apply what they know** — As we have seen above, there are many reasons competent people are not applying what they know. Another reason is because people are afraid to do the things they know. There are risks involved. If an organization does not encourage risk-taking and punishes people for mistakes, people will be afraid to try new things. New competency in terms of new skills, ideas, talents and experience will never see the light of the day in such an organization. Bright and talented people will be cowed into following the status quo. Thus, new blood and great talents will be recruited into an organization only to succumb to fear.

5) **The company has not exploited new opportunities to use new competencies** — Another reason why a company can acquire this "ailment" of unproductive competency is when it has not found new opportunities for people to use their new competency. A good example is a client who sent a group of managers to attend our training programme on "Developing Consulting Skills". Despite being equipped with the skills and knowledge, many of the participants indicated that after six months, they had yet to receive assignments that put their new skills to use. Their leaders had failed to capitalize on the new competency in this team. Their leaders could have had this team undertake some consulting work internally or carve out consulting work that will address key areas of improvements and have this team of "internal consultants" undertake the new task. By not exploiting this new opportunity, there now exists unproductive competency in the organization.

6) **The competency is of no relevance and use to the company** — Of course, unproductive competency can arise simply because the competency acquired is of no relevance or use to the company. Thus there are companies who hire people with all kinds of special skills

that they have no use for. Of course, some may argue that some of these skills may be of use in the future. The wisdom here is in the time perspective. It makes no sense to acquire skills now that are needed in five years' time since they would be obsolete by the time they are needed. There lies the need for recruiting the right people with the right set of skills at the right time. Likewise, sending staff for training in areas that are of no relevance will also be unproductive. In this case, an analysis of training needs is critical before a training plan is developed for the organization.

7) **The corporate culture prevents people from using their competency**
— Corporate culture is the way people do things in an organization. It is a set of norms comprising beliefs, attitudes, core values and behavioural patterns shared by people in the organization. A corporate culture pervades the organization to the extent that it affects policy, systems, structure, the way of thinking and strategy. For example, an organization whose culture has a low degree of risk tolerance may prevent new competencies or skills, ideas or knowledge from being applied. Likewise, a corporate culture that does not encourage individual initiative or is bureaucratic may prevent people from using their full capabilities and thus promote unproductive competency.

The key to better performance in organizations is more than just acquiring more competencies. It is about getting people to fully utilize their competencies to get better results. The role of leaders in an organization is to understand what kinds of competencies individuals have and seek ways to fully utilize them.

There are seven ways in which leaders can go about this:

1) **Provide opportunities for people to use their knowledge and skills**
— In our consulting work, we note that many leaders are not comfortable with providing people with opportunities to use their knowledge and skills. A lot of reasons that prevent these leaders from doing so are psychological and counter-productive. As mentioned earlier, some leaders fear that their subordinates will outshine them. Others do not trust their people. Yet others are afraid to delegate since they do not trust the ability of their staff. The sooner leaders realize the value of engaging people fully in achieving the goals of the organization, the faster they will achieve them. To overcome such reluctance, leaders

must first acknowledge the benefits of providing opportunities for people to use their knowledge and skills. The following are some of the benefits:

- Subordinates who utilize their skills and knowledge will perform better, and this reflects well on the leaders.
- Calling upon people to use their competency in the workplace is a way of recognizing their ability, and this helps motivate them.
- Delegating the various tasks according to the skills and knowledge of people makes the work more efficient.
- Leaders who leverage on the knowledge and skills of the staff are more effective, efficient and less stressful.
- Employees respect leaders who provide them with the opportunities to do the tasks they are good at. And with respect, leaders will have more credibility and influence.

2) **Motivate people to achieve more** — Most leaders can get people motivated to learn and build skills. However, few can really inspire people to apply their knowledge. One effective way to do this is to get each staff member to come up with a personal action plan on what they can contribute to the organization with their added skills and knowledge, each time they have been sent for a training programme. The leader's role is to guide the staff in applying their newly acquired skills. A kind word of encouragement will do wonders to reinforce the motivation to use newly acquired skills. Providing the support needed for people to apply their new skills will also boost their confidence. This may come in the form of openly endorsing the new ways and methods staff are employing in the workplace. Observing people and recognizing people's performance with positive feedback will send a strong message that the organization notices the difference individuals make in the workplace with their respective talents. The staff will know that knowledge and skills matter to the organization, and they will be motivated to translate what they know into action and henceforth bring about positive results in the workplace.

3) **Implement the better idea** — It is very dangerous for a leader to be exploring only one idea. This danger is compounded many times if that idea comes from the leader alone. To be effective in organizations, leaders must realize that they should not monopolize ideas. To get

better ideas, leaders must actively involve others in exploring ideas. They need to encourage others to think and fully utilize what they know to come up with diverse views, innovative ways and creative solutions. To do that, leaders must create an environment that allows people to speak up without fear. They must refrain from criticizing the ideas of others. They must be willing to listen to different opinions and suggestions. It is only by keeping an open mind that a leader can find better ideas. The leader must choose the better idea to implement irrespective of whom the idea comes from. To help decide on the better idea in a professional manner, a leader should set clear and transparent criteria on how an idea will be selected. The leader can weigh the pros and cons of each idea. He or she can then look at the cost and benefit of each idea along with its practicality. By professionally choosing the better idea that arises from the knowledge pool of the people, a leader fully taps into the competency of the people.

4) **Encourage innovations and risk-taking** — In the corporate environment, fear is a very significant reason for lesser performance. Many skilful, qualified and experienced executives are doing less than they are capable of because they are afraid to test what they know. Putting what they know to the test calls for doing things in a way that departs from the conventional approach. Breaking away from the status quo usually requires a bureaucratic and convoluted decision-making process. Often it is not clear what needs approval and what does not. Staff members are often confused about which particular areas they are empowered to act in and about which they are not. In many organizations, when staff members try new way of doing things, and things do not work out, the penalty can be severe. This does not encourage innovations and risk-taking.

5) **Seek out opportunities to capitalize on competency** — The purpose of developing or acquiring competency is to enable an organization to achieve its goals more effectively and efficiently. Unless leaders seek out opportunities to capitalize on the competency of the staff, the value of all the cumulated knowledge, skills and experience of the workforce will be wasted. In fact, to determine what opportunities an organization can capitalize on in the marketplace, leaders need to assess its strengths and available resources. Often, the key strengths

of a company lie in the competency of its people. Having assessed the various types of competency available in the organization, leaders should then go about capitalizing on these opportunities. For example, one of our client organizations, which is a property development business, found that over the years, their team of people had built up strong project management skills. The organization had set up a unit to undertake project management services and had been bidding for business outside the company. As a result of this, the company was able to leverage on the skills of their staff and not just the project managers only. In fact, with the new opportunity, quite a number of staff members who used to be just project members were promoted to project managers and their skills in project management could thus be fully utilized.

6) **Acquire and develop the right competency** — Unproductive competency may arise because companies recruited people with mismatched skills. It may be that the person who was hired had a set of skills that was not relevant to his job, or that the person recruited for a certain job is overqualified. This will result in knowledge and skills not being utilized fully. To solve this problem, the organization should clearly state the job specifications as well as the specific skills, knowledge and experience required. The person involved in recruitment should be briefed about these requirements and every effort should be made to hire the candidate based on the desired criteria. Of course unproductive competency can also arise if staff members are sent for the wrong training. In this case, a proper training analysis should be carried out and the right people chosen to attend training.

7) **Change your corporate culture** — One of the greatest challenges in eliminating unproductive competency in an organization is its corporate culture. There are strong elements in the corporate culture that can act as performance barriers and thus create unproductive competency. As mentioned earlier, a culture that does not encourage innovation and risk-taking may create fear in people and thus prevent them from trying new skills and knowledge in the workplace. Likewise, a hierarchically driven organization may cow capable people from volunteering new ideas and suggestions. Worst yet, it may prevent people from utilizing their knowledge and skills, and thus create unproductive competency.

The role of top leaders is to remould an organization from a hierarchic one into a performance-oriented culture. A performance-oriented culture is merit-based. A merit-based organization will assign tasks based on the knowledge and skills staff members have and not according to seniority or hierarchic position. Leaders can play an active role in changing to a more conducive corporate culture by encouraging innovation, risk-taking, empowering people, setting clear performance indicators and having a well-defined approach towards measuring performance and rewarding people.

15

The Rise of the High Performance Learning Organization

Laurence P. Smith

All organizations have to face the problem of measuring the value of training. When they send their employees for training, the costs are measurable but the benefits are unknown and not as quantitative. When it comes to the ability for organizations to sustain high performance, the odds against it are high. As a result, learning is becoming a key driver towards attaining competitive advantage over competitors.

Accenture Learning has carried out a survey involving numerous organizations to ascertain what the best Learning Organization was made of. The results revealed the seven characteristics of a High Performance Learning Organization (HPLO) and showed that only 23 of the participating 285 organizations had achieved the level of a HPLO.

HPLO helps to drive revenue and profit growth by improving productivity. The HPLO companies had all experienced a significant rise in productivity, revenue growth and net income growth, compared to their competitors and their peers.

I shall now concentrate on the seven elements or characteristics that must be in place to create a HPLO. The first two, Measurement and Alignment, are the foundation of the HPLO. Alignment is more than just a governance system. It involves the creation of a strong model that defines the roles and responsibilities towards implementing a learning strategy. It is important that the learning strategy is aligned to business needs.

There is a need to develop a system that measures and correlates training to actual business impact. Information on business impacts and job impacts are the two elements least tracked when training is conducted and evaluated. We thus see that spending on tracking and on measurement of training is small compared to the overall learning expenditure.

Another element required for HPLO companies to exist is Competency Development. The Competency Development framework includes four key areas: Learning and Development, Knowledge Management, Performance Management and Resource Management.

Learning and Development covers the delivery of controlled information and practice that can be evaluated while Knowledge Management refers to how organizations create, capture and re-use knowledge within the organization to ensure learning is maximized within the organization.

Performance Management translates corporate strategies into individual actions. This will eventually lead to continuous improvement and bring about the business result that is desired. And finally, Resource Management is the planning, deployment and management of the workforce.

Reaching the value chain is another achievement of HPLO companies. Training employees is not enough and organizations have to train the entire value chain that includes channel partners and customers. In that respect, a competitive advantage can be created if HPLO companies extend learning across the value chain and introduce Customer Offerings. This may well lead to an increase in customer satisfaction, customer loyalty, competitive differentiation over rivals, and greater product sales, and can be seen as a new source of revenue.

Integrating learning into the other daily life of the employee is an important factor to consider. Amongst others, this includes the usage of the workforce portal and the management of knowledge. Learning must also be integrated so as to allow the employee community to practise what they have been trained for.

The usage of a blended delivery approach is also another element that adds learning value to HPLO companies. By using a blended learning approach, HPLO companies gain greater cognition and higher retention, with the approach reinforcing training. Other benefits include the use of "real life" scenarios, lower costs and the benefits of individual communication and feedback.

There are numerous challenges that learning organizations face. This includes the measurement of learning to reflect its effectiveness, budget-related matters, as well as the communication of the impact of training. Human resources are assets and skills are critical, and unless organizations want to manage learning as a business, it will be difficult for them to succeed.

APPENDIX:

accenture
Learning

Evaluation Form – High Performance Learning Organization Criteria

My organization currently has the processes, tools and resources to demonstrate proficiency in the following criteria of high performance learning organizations:

1. **Alignment of learning initiatives to the business goals of the organization.**

   ☐ Strongly Agree ☐ Agree ☐ Neutral ☐ Disagree ☐ Strongly Disagree

2. **Measurement of the overall business impact of the learning function.**

   ☐ Strongly Agree ☐ Agree ☐ Neutral ☐ Disagree ☐ Strongly Disagree

3. **Movement of learning outside the "four walls" of the organization to include other members of the overall value chain such as customers and channel partners.**

   ☐ Strongly Agree ☐ Agree ☐ Neutral ☐ Disagree ☐ Strongly Disagree

4. **A focus on competency development of the organization's most critical job families.**

   ☐ Strongly Agree ☐ Agree ☐ Neutral ☐ Disagree ☐ Strongly Disagree

5. **Integration of learning with other human performance systems and functions such as knowledge management, performance support and talent management.**

   ☐ Strongly Agree ☐ Agree ☐ Neutral ☐ Disagree ☐ Strongly Disagree

6. **Blended delivery approaches that include classroom as well as both synchronous and asynchronous electronic learning.**

   ☐ Strongly Agree ☐ Agree ☐ Neutral ☐ Disagree ☐ Strongly Disagree

7. **Mature design and delivery of leadership development courses.**

   Financial Planning 70%

   ☐ Strongly Agree ☐ Agree ☐ Neutral ☐ Disagree ☐ Strongly Disagree

   Business of Company/Industry 74%

16

Performance Measurement and Management

Christopher Mills

INTRODUCTION

Academics and HR practitioners have long been absorbed with constructing the perfect performance measurement system. In the hidden depths of many leaders' minds lies the "Shangri-la" of the definitive approach to performance management. It has been re-awoken in the last decade by the resurgence of strategy-driven methodology, the process improvement culture of re-engineering, value-chain management and six-sigma, to the extent that measurement is swiftly acquiring a Nirvana-like status and becoming an additional discipline in the guise of economic value addedness (EVA), balanced scorecard, activity-based costing (ABC) and enterprise performance solutions.

The present interest in performance is therefore justified when we see that "measurement managed" companies outperform others (Schiemann & Lingle 1999).

Performance measurement and appraisal is probably the most researched area within human resources management. Agreeing on an effective method, however, has been like searching for the lost city of Atlantis i.e., hard to find. The pavements of literature are littered with discarded approaches to finding the elixir to managing employee performance.

As a result, the scroll of managing performance in the twentieth century unfolded, vacillating between setting specific directions through objectives and measuring *what* has been accomplished or by making a judgement on *how* staff has performed using traits or performance factors.

However, in the New Economy this means *Out* with boring achievement terminology such as MBO (Management by Objectives) and goals and *In* with hyped up New Economy KPIs (key performance indicators) and metrics. This also means a kick in the pants for terms that designate *how* we achieve success, such as Performance Factors and Traits, and kudos for new kids on the block terminology such as competencies and key actions.

Nevertheless in today's business environment the reality is that, "performance management" still means many things to different people. To some, it is about setting KPIs and to others, MBO, or establishing work or project plans. There are those to whom it only means Appraisal. No matter how it is described, performance management/appraisal (PM/A) has become an enigma. First personnel managers and then HR directors attempted to unravel the puzzle of putting in place a system that can make staff accountable for business performance.

A first rate performance management system should let executives craft meaningful business plans to concur on bold objectives for themselves and their staff and to monitor and react to performance requirements. This should support the attainment of strategic goals and the continued creation of value. However, do companies really operate in this manner or is it continuing to be a Nirvana?

ARE COMPANIES STRATEGICALLY FOCUSED?

A study was carried out to learn how satisfied organizations were with their current performance management/appraisal practices (Mills 2003). It was designed to audit a cross section of industries, and to establish a benchmark to facilitate effective performance management implementation. The study asked companies to give details of the measurement system they used and what was important for them in the enhancement of performance.

Since the "sense and respond" knowledge-based age challenges deep-seated approaches to managing performance, organizations seek instead to leverage their core business (De Waal 2001). However, many typically overlook the relationship between business strategy and the performance accountability of their human capital, which was why Mills' study looked at how strategically focused companies were and how they managed their performance measurement system.

This study showed that almost all companies have some form of vision or mission statement. Whether this implies that they all have a clear direction is open to conjecture. Is the vision statement displayed on the lobby walls for the sake of visitors or is it a necessary embellishment in the shareholders' report or is it a vital strategic beacon? Such questions are prompted by the study showing a steep decline after the vision. Only 27% of companies stated they had critical success factors (which lead to KPIs). 52% said their organizations had cultural values in place with only 8%

with a balanced scorecard of measures. It's rather like a chair with three legs considerably shorter. That it can stand up is doubtful.

PERFORMANCE MANAGEMENT IN THE NEW ECONOMY

What came across in this study was that all companies use their PM/A system to develop or measure individual competencies. This is not surprising since organizations have been following the competency road map and developing integrated HR models for some time (Mills 1996). It was of no surprise that "setting performance objectives" is rated highly in this study. In fact, there seems to be a correlation between companies who have staff-set objectives and companies who either are happy with their PM/A system, are about to or intending to implement a new PM/A system within 12 months, have been using a PM/A system for no more than three years, have a PM/A written policy in place, or are from a developed country.

In addition, such organizations recognize and demonstrate major aspects of a PM/A system, i.e., they are strategically focused, use competencies, provide training and have open and frequent performance reviews.

In summary, most variations occur with companies who may be changing their PM/A system soon or have no need to upgrade. Organizations more likely to be upgrading their performance system seem to see multiple benefits from PM/A.

TRENDS

As we have described, performance measurement systems have gone through a metamorphosis over the last century. Providing performance related feedback seems to be becoming common. The top three increases in future usage are predicted to be (1) team appraisal, (2) upward appraisal and (3) multi-rater feedback in that order. People need valid feedback that addresses critical competencies (skills, behaviours and motivations) required for their job and work environment (Mills 1995b). Such an exercise, although not easy to administer, helps individuals gain insight into their behaviour through the perceptions others have of their management/ leadership skills. The advantages are that hidden strengths and developmental "blind-spots" are identified.

From my own experience of going though multi-rated feedback, the benefit is that it serves as a catalyst for change. It is never comfortable hearing about areas we need to improve in that we previously thought we were alright at. However, after some reflection, we begin to buy into the need to change, which generates commitment to personal development and increases the likelihood of improved performance. In particular, it makes us more sensitive towards those we work with.

The study also highlighted a surge in the usage of performance management training. Organizations, no doubt, have fathomed that a performance-planning session or a performance review is not just about understanding how to fill in a form. They also consider the process to be just as important in ensuring consistency and calibration in measuring performance.

Top-ranked Performance Related Trends

Ranking	Performance practices	Present company usage	Future company usage	% Change
1	Team Appraisal	22%	56%	+ 34%
2	Upward Appraisal	15%	46%	+ 31%
3	360 / Multi-rater Feedback	24%	51%	+ 27%
4	Employee Training	66%	92%	+ 26%
5	Manager Training	70%	89%	+ 19%
6	Balanced Scorecard	33%	48%	+ 15%
7	Forced Ranking / Bell Curve	59%	65%	+ 6% Negative

The balanced scorecard, which has been around for over ten years, is only recently gaining ground in Asia. Undoubtedly, companies see the sense in having an "at a glance" but comprehensive framework covering financial and non-financial aspects in measuring performance. The key benefit for staff is that with the appropriate PM/A system in place, their plans should dovetail.

Future trends show an increase including forced ranking. Almost two-thirds of respondents use it, although it can prove to be a double-edged sword. The use of a method that predetermines the allocation of a percentage of employees to different categories of performance has never been popular with staff. However, what can human resource managers do when they look at their bell curve at the end of the year and find it skewed towards the high end of the rating scale? The result is an unjustified increase in budget expenditure for bonuses and payroll. What is the answer? The underlying problem lies in the assessment area of the PM/A system. The present prognosis is not encouraging without an audit of the PM/A system and the way it is used to appraise performance. In the meantime, it looks as if most companies will maintain the status quo.

SATISFACTION LEVELS WITH PERFORMANCE SYSTEMS

Organizations that are happy with the way their departments measure and manage performance have recently upgraded their systems to either performance management or a hybrid system (a system where employees set objectives and are also measured by a list of predetermined performance factors or competencies) and are more likely to use a competency-based behaviourally anchored rating (BARs) approach.

However, there is a 35% core of unhappy organizations. These are mid-sized companies, those without formal PM/A policies, those who modified their system from HQ but found that it did not work, many Japanese companies, many with trait-based systems and those with entrenched methods.

With the onset of more companies taking on a balanced scorecard and developing key performance indicators, we can conclude that measurement is becoming more important. Companies are upgrading their PM/A system to take account of setting objectives. Appraisals are likely to become more open and there is a surge of interest in training staff in PM/A practices.

CHALLENGES

Unfortunately, the challenges in the New Economy are that the same old problems in measuring and managing performance are surfacing. Still of concern is that a strategic focus for many companies merely means a vision statement. Although numerous companies have KPIs, many individual contributors still lack accurate measurement in their objectives and reliable tracking sources. Other issues include a lack of coaching on performance problems and successful use of competencies for personal development, the provision of training in the PM/A system and the development of an open, transparent system with two-way discussion at appraisal. Finally, we have the age-old issue of appraisal leniency resulting in a skewed performance bell curve to the high side with the knee-jerk reaction of forced ranking. This results in many overall ratings being lowered and much staff dissatisfaction. The final draconian step of forced ranking is always a sure sign that the performance measurement system is malfunctioning.

RECOMMENDATIONS FOR CHANGE

So why is it that such companies have not analysed the issues and upgraded the way they manage performance? Perhaps many are cautious of change and the upheaval, learning and commitment it involves. In one case, I remember the HR manager saying that his boss was responsible for introducing the present system, and so the HR manager was concerned about a loss of face for the boss if HR were to change it now. Several employees had said they were worried that a new PM/A system would threaten their jobs and affect their salary. Others feared the control factor of performance management, without realizing that it actually made work easier. However, a company that recently moved to performance management studied their staff's satisfaction level. A typical positive response was " I now know what is expected of me".

Let us imagine that we sense that there are shortcomings in the way we measure and manage performance in our company. What, then should an organization do to overcome such obstacles?

Audit your performance measurement system. The rationale advanced for a performance measurement system is that measuring and evaluating performance is central to determining the success of the business. This means that the organization needs to periodically check that the system is doing what it should.

Traditionally, human resource professionals have been responsible for driving performance systems. To gain commitment and support for change, it would seem essential to have line manager involvement in reviewing initial findings. It would also be beneficial to include selected committed non-management staff to provide another perspective. All such employees would form part of a sub-committee to make initial planning recommendations. This should involve two key steps. First, collecting data and secondly, convincing management of a need for change. The second step is much easier if you have covered your bases during the first part. This would seem to be a three-part process. It includes identifying the way forward and gaining agreement on change, understanding performance management and designing the system and encouraging follow up by monitoring progress.

One of the first things that need to be done is to examine the present approach to managing performance. This means an audit of the present PM/A system. Successful developmental efforts should include asking staff for their views on the present system. This has the advantage of getting quick feedback from all employees in a short space of time.

Firstly, data collection should be a combination of quantitative and qualitative facts and figures. Qualitative data collection entails conducting a series of focus group sessions to collect thoughts from different levels of employees. Questions on flip charts can be posted around a training room, such as: What do you like best about our PM/A system?; What do you like least about our PM/A system?; What needs to be changed and why?; What could stop the success of developing a new PM/A system? Individuals post responses and group representatives summarize key points.

Quantitative data collection is usually carried out through a study. The study should determine the following: The positive points of PM/A practices in the company; the major concerns of employees; the major frustrations staff have with the performance system; the areas we need to concentrate on when developing a new performance management system.

One could write a short note describing the purpose of the questionnaire, stating that anonymity would be respected. It is generally recommended that you target a minimum of 30% of the workforce with an equal distribution between departments and levels of staff, in order to establish validity of the data.

Preparing internal administrators to distribute and collect the questionnaires will increase the response rate. Even better, if any training course is planned then one could get staff to fill in the questionnaire at the start of the workshop. Sending questionnaires by e-mail seldom gets a good response, so that should be done only for those who must be targeted in out-of-town locations.

If the data collected suggests a need for a new PM/A system, then you can move on to Step Two.

Let us presume the results are critical of the present PM/A system. Once you know what needs to be changed, you need to get a mandate and commitment from senior decision-makers. Getting a grasp of "the business case for change" and an understanding of the pain provides a wake-up call to management and develops the conduit and foundation for transformation.

With the go-ahead for change, your inter-departmental sub-committee can start developing the new performance management system.

In one organization that I worked with, the company had identified cultural issues of teamwork and initiative that needed addressing, which their present performance system was unable to cope with. Senior executives realized that a performance management approach could be a main thrust to support this issue. This worked, and twelve months later, not only were the issues resolved but the head office also voted them the best operated company in the region. They told me that they put the increased results and cultural transformation down to the new performance management system.

AGREEING ON CHANGE AND IDENTIFYING
THE WAY FORWARD

Talented employees often drive the success of progressive companies and therefore can have a significant impact on shareholder return on investment (ROI). Exceptional staff members, like any other employee, need to determine objectives, tracking sources and attainment levels in line with KPIs and critical success factors. All these can be achieved through an effectively implemented performance management system.

Designing the System

Designing the system is like preparing a rocket for launch. You have a mission but you must first ensure the components are in place. The rocket cone is your objective section and may comprise key accountabilities, objectives, timeframes and performance indicators. A column on the form showing where employee objectives support the business plan or balanced scorecard indices helps the employee understand the importance of his/her job. This also ensures transparency of communication that scorecard goals have been cascaded down. The booster section is the area that supports and "boosts" performance. This is your competency plan comprising behavioural and functional competencies. It should have a tracking section indicating how competencies will be demonstrated.

Mid-year Performance Review

A mid-year performance review should be compulsory. It allows employees to show their results to date, how they have tracked their own performance, and get feedback from their superior on agreed performance expectations.

Appraisal and Rating Performance

Appraisal should not be viewed as a personnel exercise or a chance to justify higher pay or bonus. Appraisers should not confuse "what" the appraisees have achieved with "how" they work or vice versa or allow mitigating circumstances to be included in individual ratings. Many companies use terminology that equates with scholastic achievement, such as a five-point "A-B-C-D-E" scale where A is high. Appraisers may be expected to give "A" ratings to employees because of outstanding competencies such as spoken communication or given that their academic achievements are impressive. For example, you may have someone who has an MBA incredulous that they have been given a "C" rating on a five-point ABCDE scale where "A" is high. I remember one audit manager telling me "I've never been less than an A. In fact, with all the work I put in if I do not get an A, I'd resign". Actually, his performance just warranted a "meets expectations" rating but the company had to give him a higher rating to pacify him. This meant that the bell curve always skewed towards As and Bs. No wonder the HR department had to use forced ranking to counteract. Another person whose company appraisal scale was 1-5 where 1 is high complained to me: "My appraisal rating is a 3, I have never been lower than a 2, there must be a mistake!" In another company where I was brought in as consultant, the HR manager explained the problems she was facing. She said the performance system was not motivating superior performance from the staff and they were "just going through the motions". She said: "However, my boss does not want to change the appraisal system. He likes it because it is easy to use and everybody is familiar with it. He just wants to change the rating scale". The HR manager showed me the four-point rating scale: Good — Average — Fair — Poor. The HR manager continued: "My boss wants to put more motivating terms in the scale like 'Outstanding', 'Superior' and 'Excellent'. He thinks that was what would kick-start the staff".

Actually, it does not matter which rating you use as long as you qualify the meaning of the rating. To illustrate, let us say we have a rating scale which rates Excellent, Very Good, Good, Fair and Poor. Without clear definitions, they mean different things to different people. By specifying levels of performance, it clarifies expectations and helps with a natural distribution of results.

Definition of Ratings on a Rating Scale

Excellent	Very good	Good	Fair	Poor
Fully exceeds objective	Exceeds objective	Meets objective	Partially meets objective	Below objective

Development Planning

Many companies are now introducing development plans either as a supplement to competency assessment or as a replacement. Employees, talented or otherwise, are interested in knowing not only the development needs of their current job, but also the requirements of likely future roles.

The idea of the development plan is that it can reflect not only the development needs of the current job, but also anticipate the requirements of likely future roles and support development of culture change. It can, of course, be used as a follow-up on the areas for improvement identified in the appraisal. This overcomes the often-overheard comment: "My boss never follows up on what we talk about concerning my development". The other advantage of a development plan is that it makes the employee see that he has a "roadmap" for the future and it may increase job satisfaction. From the company's viewpoint, it can help in developing their talent pool, support potential assessment and succession planning.

Performance Management Training

Although skill development courses will play a part in many development plans, its effectiveness will often rest on the extent to which non-training solutions are found for growth. A behavioural and functional competency development guide with ideas and suggestions should be made available so that the emphasis is on "learning how to learn".

However, performance management training is essential and needs to be ongoing. It should consist of "just in time" skill-based module training to include performance planning, tracking, feedback and coaching and appraisal as well as a consistent approach to the mid-year review. Training should also have a component on personal relationship skills linked to conducting performance planning, coaching and appraisal. Ideally, each module should use the behaviour modelling process — a description of the key points, a demonstration of the concept, and practice and feedback on the participant's skill development of the concept. HR administrators also need training in the process and in how to maintain quality control over the system.

Employee Performance Handbook

An employee handbook describing the purpose, policies, benefits and processes of the system is necessary. It should feature a sample form with a completed example for planning and appraisal purposes. The process section should provide a guide towards completing a "quality" check of one's performance plan/s before a copy is sent to HR. The handbook should also describe who appraises whom and explain clearly how the rating system works to avoid misunderstanding, develop calibration amongst appraisers and hopefully, a natural distribution or bell curve.

Finally, HR needs to track success using various gauges.

Here are some examples for illustration purposes only: *Learning gauges* — 89% of all staff met performance plan quality check standards by Feb 15; *Application data* — rater consistency has resulted in a natural distribution (5% at far above expectations, 10% at exceeds expectations, 70% at meets expectations, 10% at approaching expectations and 5% at far below expectations); *Organizational change indicators* — staff met 73% of individual development targets. The total value of the performance improvements could be translated into over $2.8 million.

Encouraging Progress Follow-up

Once the new system has been through the complete performance cycle, one needs to conduct focus group sessions and complete a "post-implementation" study, rather like the one done before the system was put into place. This should help in gauging the general feeling for the system and developing a "gap analysis" to identify improvements and any key aspect that needs reviewing.

Performance Related Pay (PRP) and Pitfalls

In all such performance system reviews there is bound to be some grumbling and show of consternation that very little attempt has been made to link pay to performance, something employees tend to expect, i.e., a possible big pay rise from the new performance management system. They will ask "Was that not what it was all about in the first place?" Here is an example of a real and typical case study of the "performance-related pay" issue.

LETTER:

Hello, Chris,
I am Siew May, the new HR Manager of SLK Ltd. I have read the performance management study report thoroughly. It was very comprehensive, with many good suggestions for development. Well done. The 12-month-old system is basically good for the company and individual development. However, the priority issue from my discussions with staff is how to maximize its role so that initiatively all employees can have their salary and bonus system involved and linked to the PM system. I would appreciate it if I can get your help and support in the future on this. Looking forward to hearing from you.

REPLY:

Dear Siew May
Thank you for your e-mail and congratulations on your appointment as HR Manager.

Regarding the new performance management (PM) system, I understand your concern for a linkage to salaries. Especially as you have talked to staff and asked them their views on the system and they would have said 'It's a good system but it does not give me the money I deserve'. Right?

First of all, the system is not meant to be a pay delivery system. It is in place to link employees' responsibilities (for which they are paid a salary) to the business plan to help achieve it. If the business plan is achieved and if the person has met the expectations from the previous year they will be rewarded by another year of employment. If the company does well then they may pay a bonus but this is discretionary as is the amount the company may give as a reward to the employee.

If you really must start overtly linking pay to performance then you should review all the senior management bonusable objectives and create a process link to each position that supports each bonusable KPI.

I have put together the key points in a file 'Performance management development'. Also see the other attached article on 'linking pay to performance'. As recommended in the study I would be very happy to work further with you on the development of the system. Very pleased to be in touch with you

Best wishes,
Chris Mills

There can be problems when you link performance management to the reward system too quickly, i.e., in Year One or Year Two instead of Year Three. Here is a summary of key issues:

- Employees have high expectations of the PM system and see it as a pay delivery system and a great way to get more money.
- Employees, however, still do not have a complete understanding of the system.

- Employee objectives still need fine-tuning. KPIs call for closer scrutiny to be appropriately measured and traceable. Objectives necessitate being linked strategically to department KPIs. Some may seem difficult to measure or a strategic link may not work.
- Employees may/may not have started to use a tracking process to record their demonstration of behavioural and functional competencies.
- At appraisal time, employees fight for higher ratings, sometimes completely irrationally, just because they believe the overall rating is linked to a dollar value.
- Employees become upset when the rating does not match their feelings of self-esteem, self worth, length of service, age and educational and social standing.
- Appraisers feel uncomfortable giving less than a mid-point rating. They have difficulty justifying ratings, in particular competency-based ratings. This is because they have not collected data to back up their assumptions.
- In a good year when a company makes a profit, employee expectations are even higher and many, especially at mid/lower levels, are disappointed because their percentage increase in relation to their salary is still small.
- In a bad year when there is no profit, employees may feel it unwarranted that they are not granted a bonus, since they had put in effort nevertheless.

Performance Management

The following table recommends what is basically a three-year project plan:

Three-year Project Plan

Year 1	Introduce the system	Provide 'just in time' training in: • System design • Performance planning • Performance appraisal • Offer communication support with newsletter, performance topics, suggestions, success stories
Year 2	Develop the system	• Review issues from Year 1 and evaluate satisfaction levels Provide follow-up training on: • Measurement

continued on next page

Three-year Project Plan — *cont'd*

Year 2	**Develop the system**	• Competency tracking • Feedback & coaching • Appraiser consistency • Identify and develop PM support staff in each department. • Offer communication support with newsletter, performance topics, suggestions and success stories
Year 3	**Link to reward system**	• Provide coaching on issues from Year 2 • Identify & agree on measures and bonusable objectives/KPIs for each department • Agree on per person bonusable objectives/KPIs • Evaluate satisfaction levels/system issues • Identify key changes
Year 4	**Upgrade the system**	• Introduce new changes • Provide training where appropriate

MEASURING PERFORMANCE MANAGEMENT

Who will take responsibility for the success of the new PM/A system? What is the ROI? Performance indicators should be developed using four levels of evaluation:

- *Reaction*: How effective was the training?
- *Learning*: Do staff now understand the system?
- *Application*: Can staff create their own performance plan effectively? Can managers conduct an appraisal effectively?
- *Organizational Change*: To what extent has the organization benefited? In what tangible ways?

Here are some suggested new PM/A system performance indicators:

__% of staff rating the training as effective (where "effective"= 3 on a scale of 1–5)
__% HR personnel trained in the performance management system by____
__% of workforce trained in the performance management system by____
__% of staff submitting performance planning forms by____
__% of staff meeting quality check standards by____

__% of staff meeting 70% of individual development targets by____
__% of staff accepting the PM/A approach (where "accept" = 3 on a scale of 1–5)
__% staff rating the system as effective (where "effective"= 3 on a scale of 1–5)
__% of Department/Company goals met.

On a final note, what results should a company be looking to achieve in any future upgrade of their PM/A system? Here are some key indicators:

- Strategic focus supports critical success issues and culture change.
- Senior management switched on to their responsibilities for the success of system. Top-down modelling reinforces the importance of the system.
- Training and 1–1 planning cascade commitment to strategic objectives.
- Roles and accountabilities defined.
- Managers and staff establish reliable tracking sources.
- Coaching supports achievement of objectives and development of competencies.
- Appraisals seen as a developmental process.
- Managers not fearful of giving negative feedback and have objective data to support ratings.
- Individuals have sense of accomplishment.
- Rater consistency results in a natural distribution i.e., bell curve.
- Employees believe in the system because they have been involved and see the benefits accruing to them.
- Customer expectations measured.
- Process improvement tracked.
- Organizational development on course.
- Shareholder value increased.

Over the last hundred years, academics and HR specialists have turned the measurement and management of performance into a science by testing formula after formula in the search for the Nirvana of performance systems. Have we found such as a thing yet in the New Economy? Some may say so. We are certainly getting there with the advent of the balanced scorecard and KPIs. Why are there still skeptics? Probably because performance measurement and management implies not just a science but an art form and where success may be dependent not so much on the approach and the metrics but on the experience and leadership of those who manage the system. Given the fact that not all managers are comfortable with handling such issues, the search continues. The answer may lie in the human factor.

In summary, in the New Economy, there are and will be challenges and opportunities. If you want your company to be recognized as a top-performing organization, then fulfil your mission of measuring and managing employee performance and show an ROI on Human Resources strategic intent.

REFERENCES

De Waal, A. *Power of Performance Management: How Leading Companies Create Sustained Value*. New York: John Wiley & Sons, 2001.

Mills, C. *Under The Microscope: A study of performance management practices in Singapore*. Singapore: Singapore Human Resource Institute, 2003.

Mills, C. "High fliers or lame ducks: Are your staff competent or incompetent?" *British Business Association*. Singapore, Jan–Feb, 1996.

Mills, C. *Fact or Fantasy: A National Study of Performance Management Practices in Singapore*. Singapore: Singapore Institute of Management, 1995a.

Mills, C. "Mirror, mirror on the wall: Upward appraisal — true reflection or distorted image?" *British Business Association*. Singapore, July–August, 1995b.

Mills, C. *What's Hot What's Not: A National Study of Performance Management Practices in Malaysia*. Malaysia: Malaysian Institute of Personnel Management, 1994.

Schiemann, W.A. and J.H. Lingle. *Bullseye: Hitting Your Strategic Targets through High Impact Measurement*. New York: The Free Press, 1999.

17

Strategies to Help People Learn and Perform

Karen Ong

While evaluating factors that affect the effectiveness of training, we meet one of the main hurdles right upfront — in the classroom itself. It is hard to ignore the difference between the deep engrossment of a child in the midst of a discovery and the expressions of adult learners forced into training by corporate training plans and trapped by learning strategies that are out of place for adults.

To make learning exciting and meaningful for adult learners, Specialist Management Resources has used and promoted the FUN technique for over a decade now. FUN must balance content for results to show. FUN training, which is based on the 5 Is — Introduction, Involvement, Interaction, Instruction and Intensifying Retention — uses many techniques and tools that have enriched the toolkits of many trainers.

In this session, Karen, who has been coaching trainers and facilitators in the use of FUN techniques and tools, will present corporate best practices on the use of FUN in training. The session will use case studies to examine how the techniques have been adapted to suit varying audience needs.

Ever since the book *The Magic of Making Training Fun* by Dr R. Palan, author and international speaker, was published in 1998, we at Specialist Management Resources have made phenomenal changes in our approach to training. Fun tools and techniques have become key resources for supporting learning in our corporate and public programmes.

When we deliver training using the Fun Formula: **Fun × Content = Results**, we have had great results. Fun is a catalyst and an enabler for learning. It is a vehicle for delivering content. It is based on the five principles popularly known as Palan's 5Is.

INTRODUCTION

As with any event, how we begin our programme will determine how the rest of the session will measure up. The very first ten minutes can make or break a training session. A warm welcome with an activity-based opener can set the stage and pace for learning. Both learner and facilitator come together and begin to form a bond and rapport.

INVOLVEMENT

Learners are preoccupied with world issues outside. Involvement serves the purpose of addressing their preoccupation and getting them "ready" to receive content.

INTERACTION

Learning is not a spectator sport. Learners do not learn just by sitting in classes listening to the facilitator, memorizing pre-packaged assignments and spitting out answers. They must talk about what they are learning, write reflectively about it, relate it to past experiences, and apply it to their daily lives.

Learning in teams or learning collectively by sharing one's ideas in a group and responding to others improves thinking and deepens understanding.

INSTRUCTION

More often than not, we find that there is much content to be covered in a training session. In such situations, trainers tend to be driven by the curriculum and hence break into a continuous lecture. In fun training, alternative ways of imparting skills and knowledge include moderation of content attention management and alternatively using learner-driven methods.

INTENSIFYING RETENTION

A variety of activities is used to ensure that learners repeatedly register content that may be lost because of lack of attention paid to it. What have we gained as a result of applying the fun formula and the 5 Is?

Participants are:

- energized and charged up;
- engaged and involved;
- revitalized;
- learning and enjoying the process;
- better at retaining what they have learned, and;
- able to relate to workplace application.

Participants have communicated with us after their programmes on how the principles and formula have brought about new and exciting results that have motivated both trainer and participants.

18

Maximizing Talent for Maximizing Result

Prakash Rohera

TALENT MANAGEMENT OVERVIEW

People are the foundation for any organizational success. Individual innovations always provide the assured source of long-term success and competitiveness. Therefore, Talent Management is beneficial to both the organization and the employees. The organization benefits from (1) increased productivity and capability; (2) a better linkage between individual effort and business goals; (3) the commitment of valued employees; (4) reduced turnover; (5) increased bench strength and a better fit between people's jobs and skills. At the same time, employees tend to benefit from: (1) higher motivation and commitment; (2) career development; (3) increased knowledge about, and contribution to company goals; (4) sustained motivation and job satisfaction. For these consequences to be realized, the right people must be hired, trained, mentored and retained.

Also, today priorities have changed. Although profit is the ultimate goal of the organization, a series of paradigm shifts has been discerned, going from profit-centric organization to customer-centric models and now to employee-focused ones. Now when the employee is in the limelight, one of the major concerns of organizations is to attract, develop, motivate and retain high-potential staff. It is now recognized that such employees constitute the vital component in organization's formula for success, both in the short- and long-term perspectives.

Effective deployment and redeployment of employees is an emerging area of specialization within HR that requires solid workforce planning, analysis and skills/aptitude/interest tracking. It is essential that organizations develop the capacity to analyze their workforce and redeploy staff effectively. The typical company's growing requirements for workforce flexibility and its need to develop employee skills through developmental assignments means that people change jobs and careers inside organizations as frequently as they do between organizations.

Everyone has some special talent. However, it has to be managed and nurtured properly. Choosing, developing, motivating and retaining people with the right talents are crucial to an organization's success. Therefore, those who lead organizations today need strategies for winning the talent war.

THE TALENT WAR

The present generation of leaders has to engage and retain the people required for current and future success. One should assume that these are always in short supply. Hence, there is a struggle to rope in the best talents, and this, more than anything else, will decide whether or not an organization will win the profit war.

There are two different ways by which one can fight the talent war. One way is through the adoption of a tactic and the other through the adoption of a strategy. Tactical moves involve buying the needed talent. We may call this the headhunter alternative. The adoption of a strategy in the talent war involves on the other hand a much longer commitment to attract, develop and retain talented people.

Employees are clearly the important link. They are the knowledge workers, they are the customer interface, and they are the talents. However, the double-edged truth is that they also constitute costs. Organizational competencies reside in employees. Those who greatly exceed expectations can be classified as Stars, those employees who exceed expectations as High Potential Performers, and those who meet expectations as Performers.

The Stars are made up of high-performing and high-potential individuals who are vital to the company's future success because they have the capacity to assume greater responsibility and to manage significantly more complex tasks. These talents can also be called the crown jewels of the organization, who can help promulgate and reinforce the behavioural patterns necessary for a company to perform well. The crown jewels must be managed and developed properly for their full potential to be realized. Employees in this category are rare and would be sorely missed by any organization. They need to be reviewed, and those who stay need to experience a particular focus on their development. Some of them will not realize their potential and furthermore, the challenges that the organization may be facing now may not be what was anticipated when they were first selected.

So we come to the question: What is Talent Management?

TALENT MANAGEMENT

Talent Management is about behaviour. It is about cultivating the thoughts and actions that over time become organizational culture. Leading organizations generally view the talent management process as an ongoing, holistic and proactive exercise.

It is about identifying top talents and allocating resources to develop them in the most effective way.

While talent management in general is about all components of the workforce, including the potential workforce that exists outside the organization, it is principally an internally focused discipline. Unfortunately, most organizations tend to pay insufficient attention to internal job mobility that can boost competitiveness, increase efficiency and aid employee-retention efforts. At its core, talent management means a commitment to invest in the organization's chief asset, its human capital.

THE BUILDING BLOCKS OF TALENT MANAGEMENT

The building blocks of Talent Management are Attracting, Developing and Retaining Stars, High Potential Performers and Performers.

Attracting Talent

No matter what your business is, you cannot afford not to know whom you are hiring! The high potential staff — the Stars — are a rare breed, hard to identify and even harder to recruit and retain. Talent is always in short supply, as we noted earlier. The ability to recruit talented people is the first obvious skill to acquire if one is to have any chance of winning the talent war. Much thought has to be put into recruiting the right people and must in the end involve the allocation of time and resources. As much as anything else, the very effort put into seeking out the right talents in itself attracts potential talents. An organization that can see them as part of a strategy for its future is always attractive. Part of the overall strategy must involve means of finding out where talented people can be found, especially for senior positions. A sophisticated selection procedure should not exclude a search for talents in less obvious places.

An organization should identify talents in terms of competencies and not clones in terms of background. Tracking and monitoring external Stars can provide quick access to talent pools when a need for them suddenly arises. An organization can also source talent from synergistic institutions, which can often be a future source of Stars. Sourcing from such bodies will expand the pool of potential Stars and provide the organization with people with different perspectives.

After the organization has decided what its needs are, it must put effort into making itself attractive to talented individuals. The brand name or reputation of the organization alone may not be enough to attract top-notch talent. To convince individuals with high potential to join the organization, the support of individuals within the organization is needed, who have passion, integrity, vision, and ability to create a level of excitement that will lure them to the door. By presenting itself as tolerant and welcoming of differences, an organization can become more attractive. It must ensure that it is able to meet the needs of high-potential people.

Successful recruitment is vital in developing team members that will ensure organizational success. Selecting new employees is the most critical purchasing decision an organization can make.

Developing Stars/High Potential Performers

Beyond staffing, talent has to be managed throughout the entire employee life cycle. This means from "hire to retire". High-potential staff members who have demonstrated superior abilities, and who embody the core competencies and values of the organization should be optimally developed. Failure on the part of the organization to invest in their ongoing development almost inevitably means that their value will gradually diminish, which in turn means that they will start having less to offer the organization. If high-potential staff members are seen as a strategic response to future needs, it is axiomatic that one nurtures them to increase their value and preparedness. Learning and development, performance and incentive management, employee retention, workforce planning and worker redeployment are all part of the new workforce science.

The development of high-potential staff can be effectively done through performance management. One of the most difficult challenges an organization faces with developing and retaining high-potential talent is stringing together a range of meaningful experiences in a systematic way that will appropriately build character and skill while at the same time providing productive value to business outcomes. In order to produce a "win-win" situation, the needs of even high-potential staff must adapt to the goals of the organization.

Performance management consists of Performance Appraisal, Coaching and Counselling, Providing Rewards and Recognition.

Performance Appraisal

Performance appraisal is a system of achieving organizational goals through the review of employee performance against individual or group objectives. It can also be called Talent Review Meetings. The base for the performance appraisal system is the goals of the organization. These goals are broken down into departmental or team goals that show how each will contribute to the overall organizational goals. Objectives are then created for each position with a clear connection to the higher goals. The performance of individuals in reaching their objectives will determine whether the organization meets its goals or not. On a regular basis, usually annually or half yearly, employee performance is reviewed. This occurs for two reasons: Firstly, to reward employees for objectives met and exceeded, and secondly, to determine which objectives were not met and to develop action plans to ensure that they are achieved in future.

As part of the performance appraisal process, objectives will also be agreed on for the subsequent period. Repeated appraisals provide necessary documentation that may justify proper reasoning when an employment is terminated. When the termination is substantiated, then legal issues can be argued justifiably. They also help to determine if additional staffing is needed. Job satisfaction leads to increased productivity. Productivity enhances the quality of products. The company of course cares about how work is being done. Anyone who carries out his job accurately and efficiently saves money for the company. When the company saves money, profits go up.

It is more rational to conduct performance appraisals on a regular basis because supervisors are then able to diagnose problems early in the work process. Diagnosing problems early allows time for the situation to be reassessed at a later date to see if any progress had been made. Should the employee show him/herself to be unable to correct the problems early in the process, the supervisor can take appropriate actions to resolve the matter.

Objectives have to be measurable, and the performance requirements clearly stated. For an effective performance appraisal/talent review session, managers should prepare data for employees prior to the session. Managers need to be coached in how they can provide constructive performance feedback. Development plans need to be created and carried out for areas where objectives are not met. Objectives that are exceeded also call for rewards to be given out. In a way, the high-potential staff members are primarily responsible for driving their own development process, while the managers of these people with high potential have the specific responsibility of supporting their developmental process.

Coaching

Coaching as a developmental strategy is not a one-off thing. A good coaching process is designed to bring out the best in people, with the focus being put on business results. High-potential staff will need a succession of counsellors, teachers, coaches, and guides during the course of a successful career. Coaching key employees is becoming an increasingly popular trend. While coaching focuses on the individual, its successful implementation brings significant benefits to both the individual and the organization. These benefits include retention of valued talent, increases in productivity, development of high-potential staff, greater job satisfaction, and achievement of organization objectives. Coaching is a proven way of releasing people's mental energy. High-potential talent does not reach full development in a vacuum; rather, they are always part of, and are influenced by, corporate culture. If coaching is to be effective, it must be embraced by the organization's culture and supported by its infrastructure. Coaching is an ongoing developmental strategy. Its focus grows from orientation to the business and task in the beginning to feedback and counselling around behavioural practices geared towards building self-awareness.

Coaching possibilities for high-potential staff can be considered a company-sponsored "perk", which is also a customized developmental process intended to accelerate effectiveness at work.

Counselling

People are the most important asset of the company. The working manager or colleague can intervene in a number of daily situations that may call for professional help but that may equally be fixed through a little informal counselling.

The high-potential staff may need counselling in the following situations:

• When they are not mobilizing their energies.
• When their thinking is clouded.
• When they are not making a necessary decision.
• When they are not responding to usual motivation.
• When they are engaged in self-defeating behaviour.
• When they seem unaware of the consequences of their behaviour.

Retention

Competing for, as well as motivating, engaging, and retaining opportunity-seeking top performers should be a high priority for human resource professionals. Employers should continuously assess the right combination of reward elements to ensure that premium employees remain committed to the organization. Implementing a well-balanced mix of traditional, quantifiable elements, such as competitive salary and benefits, with more intangible rewards such as providing learning and development opportunities, is essential to the motivating, engaging, and retaining of top talent.

How to retain talent:
• Involve executive management. Company leadership should be involved in retention efforts to lend credibility to the message.
• Make HR part of the business strategy. Do not let hiring become divorced from the other activities of the firm.
• Build a culture of talent sharing. Eliminate barriers in the company culture that may keep managers from sharing their talents. That is the best way to circulate skills among departments.
• Build a talent pipeline. Establish incentives, performance metrics, and a philosophy that fosters teamwork.
• Be consistent in training and development efforts. Resist the temptation to annul these programmes to save money when times are tough.

In addition to the personal touch and appealing job content, an attractive and compelling compensation package should be offered. High Potential Performers/Stars need to see substantial upside potential based on their performance. Careful career development also has to be done for Stars to feel that they are acquiring new skills, new growth experiences and new successes that will strengthen their value, making them more marketable should their career acceleration not proceed at the rate they desire. They must feel they are moving ahead, and are respected and appreciated by the organization, and that they are adding value to the company, that they are fairly compensated, are given the support they need to be successful, and are part of an environment that is supportive and values-driven. All this will make it difficult for others to lure them away. This is admittedly a tall order for any organization to fill, but it must be addressed if the talent of high-potential staff is to be retained. Above all, they should never be taken for granted.

> ### THE TALENT FORMULA
>
> Right Strategy + Right Talent = Competitive, Profitable and Sustainable Organization

SUMMARY

People are the important assets of the company, and finding talented people is the difficult part. Identifying talent and persuading the best people that their future is with the organization are important to the company. The most difficult challenge of all can be to keep the talents a company already has from accepting another job offer. Talent will draw more talent.

There is always a talent shortage. The company with the right mix of talent and strategy will succeed, and talent management is necessary to achieve that balance. Organizations are finding that talent management — the ability to attract, recruit, motivate, develop and retain staff — is the path to success and the way to achieve customer satisfaction as well as profits.

19

How Investing in Human Capital can Translate Positively into the Organization's Performance — The Role of Benchmarking

Na Boon Chong

What this chapter highlights is the importance of benchmarking in human resource management (HRM). Benchmarking is a process of evaluating a corporation's own weaknesses and learning from top performers. It involves analysing how these top performers carry out key processes that are targeted at improving business performance and understanding the underlying reasons behind the implementation of these key processes. One must first stress the need to put a value on human capital, something that is often sidelined. There are many means for measuring HRM's contribution to business, especially in how contributions are quantified. Benchmarking is thus indispensable and much authority can be gained from quantifiable evidence in shaping HRM's processes as well as justifying its relevance and centrality to business operations.

THE VALUE OF HUMAN CAPITAL

The fact that human resources are traditionally categorized under cost in an organization's balance sheet implies that a chair is perceived as having greater value to an organisation than HR, since the furniture is listed as an asset in the balance sheet. This is ironic because physical assets depreciate over time while human assets continue to appreciate. Thus, we see the importance of quantifying contributions made by HRM to overall business goals. There is always a discrepancy between an organization's book value and its market value. A study of market-to-book ratios over time has shown that for every dollar of book value, $6 of market value is created.

The discrepancy between book value and market value is attributed to intangible factors such as human capital. Under this broad banner of human capital are factors such as leadership quality and workforce productivity, engagement and capability.

Establishing a clearer correlation between human capital and business performance is the first step in making the former more visible in the eyes of organizations hence, highlighting the importance of investing in it. There is increasing evidence that employee engagement does translate into improvements in customer service and positive financial results (see Table 1). Providing training to staff and encouraging managers to hand out recognition in known cases contributed to some intermediate successes such as better people utilization rate, service, tenure that eventually translate into improved financial successes.

TABLE 1
Some Favourable Financial and Customer Service Outcomes
Brought about by Employee Engagement

- **In ongoing research, engaged employees have been shown to:**
  - Produce $27,000 more sales per employee (Rutgers University)
  - Create $18,600 more market value per employee (Rutgers University)
  - Generate $3,800 more profits per employee (Rutgers University)
- **Impacting engagement has resulted in:**
  - Increased the rate of economic return or CFROI®, Cash Flow Return on Investment (HOLT Value Associates L.P.)
  - Reduced turnover costs at one client by $25.2 million (30%) and $5.2 million (10%) at another (Hewitt Study)
  - Increased customer retention by 5% and profitability by 25% at one client and 12% and 11.5% respectively at another (Hewitt Study)

NEW DEVELOPMENTS IN HR AND THE CHALLENGES FACING IT

HRM practices are often ineffective, lack competence and are often costly. Over the years, the role of HR has evolved. From employee champion, HR's role has expanded into administration and then to providing functional expertise. Today, the challenge for HR is to up the ante to be a strategic partner in organizations. As such, it should also be one of the team players responsible in charting a corporation's strategy and should not limit itself to being just an arm for executing strategy. Such a role requires HR to prove that it is able to help the organization achieve specific and quantifiable goals.

Table 2 examines emerging developments in demography and economy that pose a challenge to HRM. Many developed countries are faced with the issue of a greying population. Employer and employee expectations have also changed over the years. The former now expects total commitment from employees without being able to guarantee long-term employment. Simultaneously, the latter now expects the former to enhance opportunities to increase their employability through learning and development. Although employees are fully committed to organizations, such commitment is now more portable as employees are likely to have worked for more employers throughout their careers. Such developments result in uncertainty and shorter business cycles.

TABLE 2
Challenges Facing HR in the Twenty-first Century

- War for talent/labour shortage
- Demographic shift
- Change in employment contract
- Acceleration of technology; innovate to excel
- Globalization of business and network of partnerships
- Continued cost cutting/improved efficiency demands
- Heightened uncertainty

MEASURING HR'S CONTRIBUTIONS TO BUSINESS

HR has a dual role — managing HR as a cost centre as well as being a driver of organizational performance. The two observable measures of HR's functions are its activities and costs. However, from a business perspective, HR will be assessed by how it contributes to business success. HR professionals who are still operating at the low end of the value chain excel in traditional roles as employee champion but are limited in distinguishing themselves in other ways. Most importantly, such professionals are often incapable of linking their expertise to bottom-line results that are observable and that the organization can appreciate and evaluate. As such, HR must find a better way to measure its contribution to the business. It needs to be innovative in measuring outcomes that clearly demonstrate the impact on the workforce (Table 3).

TABLE 3
Changing the Measures of Performance —
Value of HR for the Twenty-first Century

- Value of HR for the twenty-first century
  - HR with an attitude: Be catalyst for change and take initiative to lead.
  - Turn knowledge into action, activities into outcomes.
  - Keep sharp eye on business results.
  - Make decisions based on deep understanding of the business.

Measuring this value

⇩

- Shift measures to reflect future work; scorecard focused on workforce versus operational measures
  - Productivity
  - Engagement and environment
  - Performance management
  - Talent deployment

The trend is now for HR to function with a smaller budget. The HR professional to full-time employee (FTE) ratio has also increased from 1 to 100 to 1 to 250. In addition, more HR functions are also now being outsourced and HR is now expected to demonstrate the returns on technology investment in as little as 12 months. Thus, since HR is moving up the value chain, it also needs to ensure the high standards of its daily instructions and cannot afford to slacken in performing such roles. As such, there are six essential ways for HR professionals to deal with the new realities outlined above. HR professionals need to:

- Know the reality in quantitative terms.
- Know the market like a marketing person.
- Know costs like a finance person.
- Know technology like an IT person.
- Know partners or potential partners like a business development person.
- Know HR business, like a chief executive officer or a general manager of HR.

Some quantifiable ways of measuring HR are:

• HR's expenses as a percentage of total expenses.
• HR staff to FTE ratio.
• HR cost per employee.

In addition to knowing internal customers, HR must also be knowledgeable about external talent market. Whilst internal customers' views can be obtained through a proper survey, there is a means developed by Hewitt — called a HR Catalyst Tool — specifically for this purpose. Another expedient way of measuring this is to add some additional questions on internal customer priorities into the existing regular employee survey and then using a 2 by 2 or 3 by 3 matrix on the whiteboard to plot the priorities and assess HR's effectiveness in meeting these priorities. Such an exercise would provide useful feedback and help HR professionals to plan HR agenda.

One could assess HR costs by charting a detailed activity-based costing project (Figure 1) or through a simple in-house exercise.

FIGURE 1
Know Your Costs/Returns Like You are a Chief Finance Officer

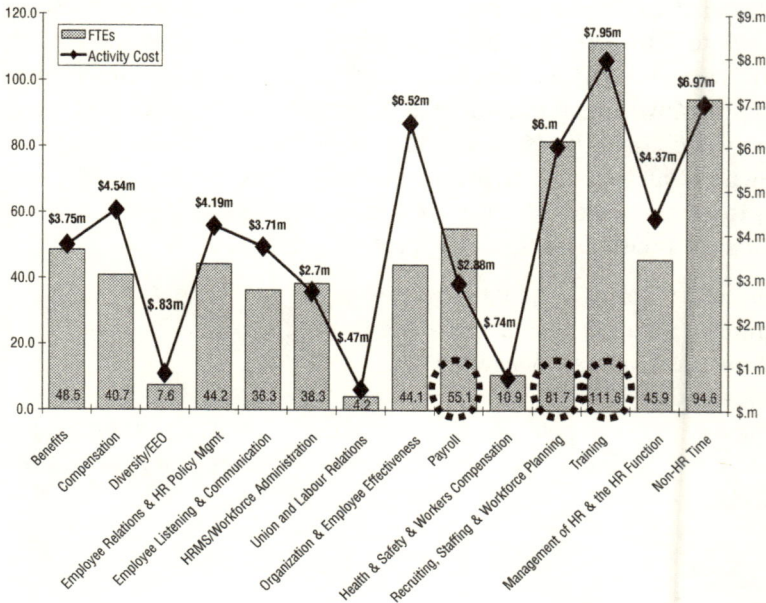

HR professionals need to know in detail the plethora of technology available for HRM in order to make decisions on which ones should be tapped into. Moreover, there is a need for professionals to have a full understanding of the likely impact of various technologies, the ROI of a particular technology, the particular technology that can be introduced in-house and whether the services of a partner is required. However, when the day comes for all HR activities to be outsourced, HR professionals will then have to be capable of managing vendors and projects in addition to providing strategic advising and relationship management. As such, HR professionals must be equipped with knowledge to make the following assessments:

- Which vendors are worthy partners?
- What value will they bring?
- What synergies can be expected?
- How will this impact on business performance and profitability?
- What skills are needed for cooperation with chosen vendors?

With regards to knowing a business like a chief executive officer, HR professionals need to link HR values creation with business values creation — covering both business performance and business costs. As such, HR professionals should have answers to the following questions:

- What business are we in?
- What is core/what is non-core?
- Which parts of our business are creating value, or making/losing money?
- What services would we provide?
- Which areas should we build?
- Where should we seek partners?

THE POWER OF QUANTITATIVE EVIDENCE

Our general experience in dealing with clients is that quantitative evidence boosts the decision-making process. This is because quantitative evidence makes real problems more visible thus making it easier to focus on them. Hewitt's research also shows that internal resources and anecdotal evidence do not allow rigour and dampen decision-making process. As such, all quantitative evidence should be gathered within a month to leave more time for discussion and analysis. In addition, the availability of quantitative evidence allows HR professionals to respond to tough questions that are often posed by chief executive officers and chief finance officers:

Q: What return are we getting on our investment in people?
Quantitative evidence: Human capital rate of investment, HR revenue percent and HR expense percent.

Q: What does it cost our company to deliver HR services?
Quantitative evidence: Total HR cost percent.

Q: Is our overall HR budget (capital and operating) appropriate, given our current HR design, HR strategy, and business environment?
Quantitative evidence: HR expense percent, HR expense factor, HR staff to FTE ratio, HR cost per EE.

Q: Are we spending our money on the activities that will help drive our business?
Quantitative evidence: Percentage time by activity, percentage time by activity type and total HR activity cost per employee.

Hewitt's research shows that quantitative evidence also facilitates informed decision-making in re-engineering HR processes in the quest to develop an optimal HR operating model and make outsourcing decisions.

There is therefore a need to price HR services if it is to operate as a business. Pricing must cover a few components, starting with the direct cost of providing services, use of partner such as insurance carrier, payroll outsourcing vendors, training service vendors and corporate allocation to HR. The ultimate target of pricing HR services is to attach a premium to the value as perceived by the internal customers. A threshold price level should break even without premium and with zero contribution to overheads, i.e., covering the direct costs. Alternatively, it can be discounted from full cost recovery but with some contribution to overheads. Activity analysis is the fastest and most advanced method of analysing the HR business.

CASE STUDIES OF A FEW EARLY LEARNERS

Here, we can cite four case studies of corporations that have embarked in adopting activity analysis and observable benefits enjoyed by these corporations after doing so:

Case Study #1 — Siemens

The corporation has so far achieved $15 million in savings with more savings on the way. Its activity analysis reveals that:

- there are many redundant HR processes despite outsourcing benefits administration;
- too many staff members were still answering benefits questions, and;
- HR is overstaffed at divisions of business units, leading to inconsistent processes and information provided to employees.

Case Study #2 — Verizon

The corporation has so far achieved 18% of the savings targeted for the year. Its activity analysis reveals that:

- it spends $53,000,000 or more than 20% of HR budget on managing transactions;
- significant HR resources are used to answer routine questions related to "outsourced" functions;
- employees don't know where to go to get answers to basic questions about HR programmes and policies, and;
- six key areas need improvement.

Case Study #3 — Ahold

The corporation has so far achieved $7 million in savings. In addition, its ROI is targeted to exceed 140%. Its activity analysis led to:

- a redefinition of HR delivery model to match business model;
- an implementation of uniform technology platform including user-friendly, reliable HR applications;
- a re-engineering of over 140 HR processes;
- a business case for HR transformation built on savings from 1% reduction in turnover, and;
- a centralized payroll and HR data management and aggregated payroll vendors.

Case Study #4 — Philips

The corporation is expected to achieve $60 million in savings over a five-year period. After its activity analysis, the corporation:

- identified various savings opportunities;
- implemented regionally deployed HR shared services for their North America, Pan European, and Pan Asian regions;
- outsourced non-core functions region by region, and;
- consolidated business unit HR activities into shared services and saved costs.

BENCHMARKING

Benchmarking is strongly recommended for those who are ready for change. However, we must remember that benchmarking does have its advantages and disadvantages:

Advantages

- External focus
- Proactive
- In-depth
- Leading industry
- Breakthroughs

Disadvantages

- "Keep up with the Jones"
- Form over substance
- Nibbling at the peripheral and missing the strategic levers

Table 4 outlines the desired end-state of benchmarking.

TABLE 4
Desired End-state of Benchmarking

	From	To
Points for Comparison	Self-perpetuating formal programmes.	Self-reflective learning process.
Focal Point of the Process	Produce a written document. Control implementation through budgets and programmes.	Simulate strategic thinking. Foster organizational learning. Coordinate executive action.
Evaluation Criteria	Historical: Current performance is compared to previous organizational performance.	Strategic: Competitors' performance levels and market characteristics (for example, growth demand, innovativeness) provide standards for assessing performance.
Modes of Interaction	Formalized and numbers-oriented. Discussion centres on incremental adjustments from year to year.	Information, word-oriented, self-reflective. Discussion centres on exploring managers' understanding of mental models and assumptions, strategic issues and the feasibility of proposed solutions.
Managerial Attention	Directed towards operational issues of a business. Defending current competitive position.	Directed towards "strategic frontiers" of current business. Prospecting for new opportunities.

CORPORATE EXPERIENCES

20

Finding, Nurturing and Developing the Professional Workforce — The BSP Experience

Gary Young

INTRODUCTION

The tag-line that "people are our greatest assets" has been heard time and time again in the popular media. Peter Drucker, often regarded as the father of modern management, reinforced the importance of human assets when he said that " the single most important competitive advantage will be…the ability of a company to attract, hold and motivate workers…".

Nevertheless, retrenchment, redundancies and job cuts are equally everyday news. In this situation, do workers actually believe that they are treated as if they were the firm's greatest assets? Is it all lip service?

This paper looks at the experience of Brunei Shell Petroleum Company (BSP) in attracting and developing its professional workforce. It is hoped that our experience goes some way towards at least giving our employees, Bruneians and expatriates alike, a real sense that they "make a difference" in building a competitive edge for BSP.

BSP PEOPLE STRATEGY

The current BSP People Strategy was crafted in 2001. This strategy puts the balance between local and global needs at its centre by putting emphasis on the following:

- The aspirations of the nation will drive our Bruneianization policies, while we at the same time wish to be an employer of choice for both locals and foreigners.
- The use of global competence-based development (CBD) tools and processes to ensure a level playing field.

- The recognition of professional qualifications that meet international standards.
- The importance of maintaining an international flavour in our workforce.
- The increasing use of international assignments for Bruneians to develop their skills and leadership.

A clear aspiration for the future is to equalize the number of Bruneians working abroad with the number of expatriates working in BSP. Given that we have been a net importer of labour since the very beginning, this is indeed a tall order, but one that gives tremendous impetus to our development initiatives.

BSP'S HUMAN RESOURCE DEVELOPMENT APPROACH

Four key principles decide the way we approach human resource development:

- Personal development and career management are increasingly placed in the hands of the individual.
- Greater recognition that functional/technical skills build the professional (what you are) while behavioural/life skills build the person (who you are).
- Competence-based development and competence-based progression using global minimum standards and processes, which take into consideration performance and local requirements, will increasingly characterize the way we address human resource planning and development.
- A re-focus on our core values and Enterprise First behaviours (described later in this paper).

FINDING HIGH CALIBER GRADUATES

BSP has employed a "grow our own timber" strategy for many years by allocating significant investments in the education system and more particularly in sponsoring scholarships for young and bright Bruneian school leavers.

In the field of education, BSP is active in contributing expertise and resources. Examples include our sponsorship of a masters degree in the geosciences at the University of Brunei Darussalam, the setting up of the Oil and Gas Discovery Centre to spur interest in science and mathematics amongst schoolchildren, and many others. The main challenge in finding graduates of the right quality has always been the small pool of suitably qualified students eligible for scholarship selection to undertake technical study disciplines such as in geophysics and petroleum engineering. Figures show that in the last ten years we averaged between only 10 to 12 scholarship awards per year.

Direct recruitment of Bruneian graduates from the open market has traditionally been low, in the order of six or less per year. However, since 2000, we have had a greater degree of success in open market recruitment, in the order of 20 to 24 per year. This strongly reflects the fact that degree qualifications are becoming more affordable and accessible. In the last four years we have been receiving about 180 applications from graduates per year. Our selection process starts with a check that qualifications are in the relevant fields and of at least lower second level classification. Some 25% of all applications received make it through to the next stage, which is the assessment centre. In an assessment centre, applicants are put through three rigorous exercises designed to reveal their qualities of Capacity, Achievement and Relationship. Only about 10% pass the assessment centre stage. The final stage is the interview.

Given the numbers above, it is clear that resourcing the organization with 30 new graduates per year, which is our target, is indeed challenging.

DEVELOPING OUR GRADUATES INTO COMPETENT NEW PROFESSIONALS

Bruneian graduates enter working life with certain characteristics. Since most have never worked before, they require much help and support in their initial years. They also tend to need help in developing personal skills. For these reasons, the first three to five years are very critical. Our initial objectives for the graduates are, clearly, to ensure:

- a smooth transition into the working environment;
- rapid professional contribution;
- demonstration of personal effectiveness, and;
- alignment with and embedding of the required values and behaviours.

All technical graduates follow a Graduate Development Framework (GDF) that outlines their development responsibilities and priorities during their first three to five years.

The framework is integrated with several key human resource processes such as probation, confirmation in employment, transfer to an established position and early career review. Non-technical graduates such as those in finance and HR, for example, follow similar guidelines laid down by their respective professional discipline.

All graduates are required to attend a graduate induction programme organized by the Learning and Development Department within six to twelve months of entry. Understanding more about the business and organization that they have joined makes up a large part of the agenda. At the same time, they begin the process of developing responsibility and accountability, especially in matters such as personal development and career management.

Key messages imparted by senior business and HR leaders include the following:

- Learning is a continuous activity and lifelong learning is essential;
- Everyone needs to acquire a mix of capabilities in order to be successful;
- Leaders must learn to teach others, and;
- Work on the level of motivation and on the adopted attitude.

Other advice we give includes the "3×3 guide": If you wish to grow, then you need to (1) take your personal development seriously; (2) get out of your comfort zone, and; (3) find resources for your growth. If you wish your career to blossom, then (1) network like crazy; (2) be credible, and; (3) be visible.

DEVELOPMENT OPTIONS

The diagram below shows the four different ways in which personal development takes place. In BSP, all four modalities play a role in our HRD effort.

Off-the-job learning experience	INSTRUCT	EXPOSE
On-the-job learning experience	SUPPORT AND COACH	MENTOR

| | Incremental change | Transformational change |

SUPPORT AND COACH

Learning primarily happens on the job, and is often regarded by practitioners and trainees alike to be the most effective way to learn.

A pedagogical approach to many years of schooling however tends to imbue a sense of passivity to learning on the part of the students. Sometimes, this is referred to as the spoon-feeding approach. It is very important that our graduates realize that they must manage their own learning and not leave it for the system to take care of.

Support and coaching are key competence development mechanisms available in the workplace. In BSP, the capability support network is well established. For example, a technical graduate working in the subsurface skill pool will be able to find resources such as his/her supervisor, discipline leader, colleagues, team members, capability coordinator, global network colleagues etc. Oftentimes, the young graduate is quite unaware of these learning resources around him/her.

INSTRUCT

Off-the-job learning, i.e., attending a formal training programme off the worksite, is an important way to close competence gaps among the staff. BSP runs a large training department housed in a modern facility in Seria where many learning programmes take place every year. Programmes are run by in-house resources as well as resources from Shell Group and third parties. On average, every BSP employee takes between five to eight days of formal training per year. The direct training investment per employee works out at approximately B$4,000 per year. These are significant investments in the development of our staff, well benchmarked with other Shell operating companies.

MENTOR

A powerful way of personal learning is mentoring. In mentoring, a relationship is set up between a senior and more experienced person known as the mentor, and a younger member of staff known as the mentee. The purpose of the relationship is to help the mentee learn from the experience of the mentor.

A "life skills" mentoring scheme is in effect in BSP, and has the following objectives:

- Embed mentoring as part of the people development culture;
- Train our leaders to be mentors;
- Ensure that our graduates develop life skills along with functional skills, and;
- Contribute towards BSP's business objectives

A programme manager is in place to monitor and provide support. Some fifty mentors are currently paired with 103 graduate mentees.

PROVIDE EXPOSURE

Exposing staff to a new environment offers a vast scope for new learning. Since Shell operates in many countries and cultures, many opportunities for international postings are available and are much sought after. Targeted developmental assignments via cross-postings in line with career progression plans help staff to acquire the breadth of experience necessary for higher-level positions in the organization.

The Shell Group makes use of several mechanisms to facilitate international postings. The most common is International Open Resourcing. Job vacancies are posted on the Shell Wide Web, allowing applications to be received from eligible staff in any part of the world. The system theoretically enables the best and most suitable candidate to be found.

Given that jobs are becoming scarcer and the competition higher, Bruneians wishing to embark on an international posting obviously need to be at least on a par in terms of capability with their global counterparts. This is where having a single CBD system helps.

Our annual target is for twenty staff members to embark on international assignments. In the last four years, we have achieved 13–16 postings aboard. By December 2004, 59 staff members were working aboard. Their experience will greatly assist in providing the leadership skills much needed by BSP in the future.

GLOBAL COMPETENCE-BASED DEVELOPMENT (CBD)

Shell launched a global CBD framework with associated tools and processes in 2003. Such a global system has several benefits. It puts in place a common language, and is transparent, fair and consistent.

First and foremost, CBD is about the development of the individual. Through the definitions of competencies in a hierarchical structure — expertise area, skill building blocks, skill elements, and a global competence scale — it is now possible for any professional staff member to identify his or her gaps against a target job profile, and agree on these gaps with the coach or supervisor so that a proper development plan can be pursued. By closing these gaps through a rigorous assessment process, the individual builds up capability and becomes eligible for further progression consideration. Processes for both development and progression are globally adhered to.

LEADERSHIP CHALLENGES

In striving to grow, BSP's leaders face some considerable challenges, such as those outlined below:

- Sustaining workforce motivation;
- Dealing with complex and sophisticated issues such as globalization and inclusiveness;
- Demonstrating core values in everyday behaviour;
- Bridging the leadership credibility gap, and earning trust and loyalty;
- Coping with the needs of a changing workforce that is more educated, has shorter-term focus, and more ready to protest, and;
- Seeking higher levels of performance from the staff.

Shell's leadership framework is euphemistically named the Nine Planets, so-called because there are nine key leadership competencies or abilities. These are listed below:

1. Building shared vision.
2. Championing customer focus.
3. Maximizing business opportunities.
4. Demonstrating professional mastery.
5. Displaying personal effectiveness.
6. Demonstrating courage.
7. Motivating, coaching and developing.
8. Valuing differences.
9. Delivering results.

A full suite of group-wide programmes is available to satisfy the needs of all, ranging from young graduates all the way to senior and experienced leaders. The delivery faculty includes the likes of INSEAD, IMD and Wharton business schools.

Underpinning all our leadership initiatives is an emphasis on Shell's core values — honesty, integrity and respect for people. These values have become all the more relevant today.

Enterprise First behaviours — leadership, accountability and teamwork — are physical manifestations of our core values. It is hoped that the cultural change brought about through the implementation of Enterprise First initiatives will quickly spur Shell towards its former top quartile performance ranking and bring other long-term benefits.

KEY PEOPLE DEVELOPMENT CHALLENGES

Four specific challenges can be identified. First, there is the need to maximize returns from the large investments we currently make in off-the-job learning. This will entail more rigorous pre-course and post-course preparation and evaluation, as well as the tracking of learning KPIs. Second, much more effort is required to establish fully a culture of self-managed learning in the organization. This means that the staff must be more proactive, and coaches and supervisors must support the learning process by integrating work objectives with learning objectives.

Third, we have to realize that functional skills alone are insufficient. They have to be supplemented with broader business skills. There is much wisdom in the saying that "if you only know how to use a hammer, every problem will look like a nail". Fourth, from an organizational perspective, we need to re-establish career ladders for technical specialists. Not only will this motivate technical staff in progression terms, the company will benefit from keeping highly valued skills from being eroded.

THE BRUNEIANIZATION SUCCESS STORY

BSP's continuous efforts in the human resource development field have already reaped enormous benefits. The existing strong and long relationship between Shell and its partners in the Brunei government creates a platform of trust and respect.

Over the last 20 years, BSP has seen a dramatic turnaround in the composition of its staff. In 1984, fully three quarters of its professional staff were foreigners, and 17% were local citizens. By the end of 2004, the reverse had become the case — 70% were now citizens and foreigners made up 27%. In the junior staff category, the citizen category has grown from 55% to 91%.

A more telling statistic is the composition of the leadership positions of the company, from department heads and above. Citizens now hold 58% of these positions. Two of the five senior directors are Bruneians. BSP will continue to direct efforts towards nurturing our leaders, and embedding a healthy and positive company culture based on best practice HRD.

21

Learning Strategies for Global Competitiveness: The Petronas Experience

Putri Juliani Johari

Learning is a key competency to success. One has to keep on learning in order to achieve one's goals and to positively contribute as a team player in a company. Learning itself can provide the catalyst and the intellectual resource to create a sustainable competitive advantage for many organizations. Such is the case for market champions — entities who strive on continuous learning, and who continue to learn how to do things better. At Petronas, the adoption and implementation of learning strategies have been very successful.

Petronas, or Petroleum Nasional Berhad, is Malaysia's national petroleum corporation. Since its incorporation in 1974, Petronas has transformed itself into a fully integrated multinational petroleum corporation with business interests in more than 30 countries. Petronas has embraced the fact that learning *how to learn* can positively contribute towards the success of developing human resources. Correct learning strategies, coupled with correct training or teaching strategies, when implemented, are the key competencies for sustaining global competitiveness. To necessitate this, trainers and learners together have to know the principles required to achieve these strategies, and to be able to translate such principles into practice.

Often, companies need to realign their business direction, and so the current workforce needs to be trained quickly in order to face challenging business demands. *Re-skilling* is not just a new fad; it is an important recipe for success in human resource development, as new knowledge is constantly needed to solve new on-site problems. For big multinational companies such as Petronas, this is not only a business reality — it is a business priority. Petronas has recognized that to enable performance to be achieved at the required standard, competence should be seen as a combination of awareness knowledge, skills and attitude. The company thrives on its human resource mission statement, i.e., "We want to develop people who are *Capable, Confident* and *Committed* and develop a *Challenging, Attractive* and *Conducive* environment". There are indeed many young employees working at the company, and Petronas encourages, through scholarships and education, bright students right from the high-school level to be knowledgeable in the company's functions and roles. Such selected students are groomed and moulded by the company to be the next generation of experts and executives, with a chance to climb the corporate ladder within the company. With the company mission in mind, the right kinds of people are produced from the start, to be integrated and fused into the successful processes of the company.

The key element of success for Petronas is *performance*. The performance of employees is constantly monitored and measured, and it is the job of the human resource developers to intervene when they notice cases who do not perform and who are non-productive. Performance is indeed viewed very seriously by the company, which rightfully explains the heavy investments that Petronas puts on providing its people with opportunities for continuous learning and training. Petronas adopts a total approach to learning; it takes into account the myriad of parties involved in the learning process — the various learning providers, trainers and educators, employees, and leaders, to name a few. Staff members are encouraged to grab such opportunities, and leaders are required to make time for their staff. This is because it is important to understand that the individual (the staff) is the actual driver of the learning process, and not the leader or manager.

The investments put into educating Petronas employees are evident in the numbers trained and the quality of the training, learning and development centres that have been created over the years. One such centre is Permata, one of the two training institutions operated and managed by Petronas Management Training Sdn. Bhd., which is a wholly owned subsidiary of Petronas. Permata takes pride in its motto, "Your learning partner of choice", and it functions by teaching and training employees in management skills, leadership, and competency development. Other learning providers of Petronas include Alam, which handles all the maritime education and training of the employees, UTP, Petronas' very own university that aims to produce well-rounded graduates, INSTEP, a centre for teaching training, skills and competency development, and OPUS, the operating units that provides the environment and practical simulations for actual on-the-job training. These centres all have one goal in mind — to attain and sustain Petronas' corporate agenda, which is to become a global champion. In a study done by Permata, a large percentage of the employees surveyed mentioned that they were ready and willing to move forward in the company. This means that they were motivated and driven to succeed and climb higher on their job ladder, and for Petronas to provide such opportunities, especially learning opportunities, is a phenomenon worth copying.

The education division of the company has put an emphasis and a significant shift in its views on education, i.e., from focusing too much on *training*, to instead increasingly stressing on *educating*. This shift provides a framework for becoming more "learner-centred" as opposed to "trainer-dependent", from "compulsory learning" to "self-directedness", and from "one-off events" to "continuous learning". The education division also takes pride in its own brand essence — inspiring others in lifelong learning. In fact, their vision statement is "Champion for continuous learning and development of intellectual capital", where the greater emphasis on the shift from training to learning is furthered through the incorporation of a need for greater effectiveness in developing and upgrading skills and competencies. This is "continuous learning, from the cradle to the grave". For example, the company not only grooms younger generations to become experts and professionals for the benefit of the organization in the future, it also prepares current staff for retirement, educating them in ways that allow the employees themselves to realize their own potentials and their abilities to contribute economically even after their retirement.

The competencies needed by the company that are to be achieved by its people encompass skill development for everyone. This includes a sense of awareness, knowledge, and skills that provide independence and minimizes micro-management. These competencies are mandatory in the company, and an inability to achieve them makes an employee non-promotable. There are indeed different tiers of competencies that can be achieved according to the different levels of work categories and sectors.

However, the most important aspect in achieving these competencies is *learning*, and their role as learning providers and human resource developers in Petronas is to train and educate not only the employees but also the training facilitators themselves. Although learning does not come from the facilitator but from the learner himself or herself, it is equally important that the learning providers know what they are saying.

Finally, some guiding principles that may be useful to trainers in human resource development, and that are practised at Permata include intensive research, the soliciting of feedback, a focus on interaction and the derivation of high energy in classes, personal development focus versus team participation, largely familiar ground and supported by grounded theories and concepts, and excellent support and reception at all levels.

About the Authors

TUN DR MAHATHIR MOHAMAD joined active politics in 1945, and was first elected as a Member of Parliament in the 1964 General Elections. In 1973, Dr Mahathir was appointed a Senator. In 1974, he became Minister of Education. In 1976, he was appointed Deputy Prime Minister in addition to his Education portfolio. He relinquished the latter in January 1978 for that of Trade and Industry. Dr Mahathir was elected an UMNO Vice-President in 1975. In 1978, he became the party's Deputy President. On 16 July 1981, he became the fourth Prime Minister of Malaysia, and retired from the post on 31 October 2003.

He is the author of several books, including *The Malay Dilemma, The Way Forward, The Challenge, The Malaysian Currency Crisis* and *Globalisation and the New Realities.* He has also written several books about issues affecting the Muslim world, including *The Role of Islam in The Modern State* and *Islam and the Muslim Ummah.*

At present, he serves as Adviser to four government entities, namely Petroliam Nasional Berhad (Petronas), Perusahaan Otomobil Nasional Berhad (Proton), Langkawi Island Development Authority and Tioman Island Development Authority.

PEHIN DATO HJ AWANG ABDUL AZIZ UMAR is the Minister of Education of Brunei Darussalam. He also plays significant roles in various government councils such as The National Legislative Council, The Privy Council, The Council of Ministers, The Council of Succession and The Islamic Religious Council. He has a distinguished career in numerous fields, especially in infrastructure development, education, health and communications.

After attaining a Bachelor of Social Sciences degree in Economics, Politics and Sociology in 1964, he served as an administrative officer and then directed departments such as Public Works and Establishment. In 1973, he became State Secretary and was promoted in 1981 to Acting Chief Minister. He has held many offices within the Brunei Darussalam government service, particularly as Minister of Education and Health,

Acting Minister of Health, President cum Chairman of Southeast Asian Ministers of Education Council (SEAMEO Council) and Chairman of Brunei Investment Agency.

He has received various awards and decorations obtained from Brunei Darussalam, Jordan, the United Kingdom, Pakistan and Thailand, and has been conferred many honorary doctorate awards from various renowned international universities and Universiti Brunei Darussalam, such as Honorary Doctor of Laws awarded by the University of Liverpool and Fellowship of The Royal College of Surgeons from The Royal College of Surgeons, Edinburgh.

GÜNTER K. STAHL is Assistant Professor of Organizational Behaviour at INSEAD and was Assistant Professor of Leadership and Human Resource Management at the University of Bayreuth (Germany) and visiting fellow at the Fuqua School of Business and the Wharton School of the University of Pennsylvania (USA). At INSEAD, Stahl has been teaching MBA, Executive MBA, and Executive Development Programmes. In addition to this, he was involved in the design of innovative management development systems for various multinational corporations.

Stahl has (co-) authored several books, including *Developing Global Business Leaders: Policies, Processes, and Innovations* (Quorum Books), and many journal articles and teaching cases. He has received several research awards, including the Carolyn Dexter Best International Paper Award of the Academy of Management and the Academy of Intercultural Studies and Daimler Chrysler Award. His current research interests include the link between strategy and leadership, global leadership development and international career issues, the dynamics of trust within and between organizations, and the management of mergers and acquisitions. Stahl is also co-editor of the *Handbook of Research in International Human Resource Management* (Edward Elgar), and principal investigator for the Asia-Pacific region of the "Global Human Resource Management Research Alliance".

DAVID SCRUGGS is Vice President of Dale Carnegie & Associates, Inc. and the Curriculum Director for Leadership Development in the Dale Carnegie Global Services Department headquartered in St. Louis, Missouri. He managed the Asia Pacific and African regions for Dale Carnegie and Associates from 1996 through 2001.

David has been with the Dale Carnegie organization since 1986. He is a Master-Trainer in all Dale Carnegie programmes and seminars. He has supported Dale Carnegie's franchise development worldwide in over 30 countries, working with franchisees and their clients to develop local trainer capabilities, global partnerships and strategic relationships. Some of the new Dale Carnegie franchises and territories that he has played a key developmental role in opening include Malaysia, Mauritius, Kenya, New Zealand, Beijing, Mumbai, Delhi and Brunei.

ROBERTO F. DE OCAMPO is president of the Asian Institute of Management. Between 1992 and 1998, he served as Secretary of Finance under President Fidel V. Ramos and was widely recognized as the principal architect of the resurgence of the Philippine economy. He graduated with honours from De La Salle College (1962) and the Ateneo de Manila University (1967) where he received his Bachelor of Arts in Economics (Cum Laude). He has a Master in Business Administration from the University of Michigan (1970) and a post-graduate diploma from the London School of Economics (1971).

He began his career in public service in 1972 by initiating the rural electrification programme. He received the Ten Outstanding Young Men of the Philippines (TOYM) award in 1975. After working as a senior loan officer at the World Bank, he was appointed chairman and CEO of the Development Bank of the Philippines (DBP) in 1989. He was presented with the very first "Man of the Year Award" by the Association of Development Finance Institutions in the Asia-Pacific (ADFIAF) in 1997.

In 1995, he was named "Finance Minister of the Year" by *Euromoney* magazine, the first Filipino and first ASEAN finance minister to be so recognized. He was chosen in 1996 by Euromoney as "Finance Minister of the Year", and in 1997, he was again cited as "Asian Finance Minister of the Year", this time by the *Asiamoney* magazine.

DR R. PALAN is Chairman of Specialist Management Resources Group, a company with a 27-year track record. The company is involved in ER training, consulting & technology. Palan's 5 Is — Introduce, Involve, Interact, Instruct, and Intensify Retention are based on theoretical models and extensive research. Before he became a full-time consultant, he was the Marketing Director/Chief Executive Officer of a large resort hotel. He served one term as the Chairman of the Working Committee on HRD, ASEAN Chamber of Commerce and Industry.

He holds a Bachelor's degree in Chemistry from New College, University of Madras and a Certificate in Plastics Technology from the institute of

Plastics Technology, Madras. He then pursued his Masters focusing on Social Sciences at the Madras School of Social Work. Later, he pursued his Certificate in Personnel Management and Industrial Relations from the Malaysian Institute of Management. He completed his Ph.D. in Organizational Behaviour with the California Coast University, Santa Ana. He also attended Harvard Business School, the John Anderson School at the University of California, Los Angeles, and the National Training Laboratories.

He has authored several books, including *Competency Management: A practitioner's guide, Frequently Asked Questions in Human Resources Development, Performance Management & Measurement: The Asian context, The Magic of Making Training FUN!!, 101 Frame Jokes, Creating Your Own Rainbow* and *Creative Training Tips*.

DAVID CORY is a workplace performance consultant specializing in individual and organisational performance improvement. In addition to a Master of Arts Degree in Adult Education, David is certified as a trainer/ facilitator with Achieve Global, Development Dimensions International (DDI), Gilmore, and Insights. He is a Certified Trainer in the area of Emotional Intelligence (E1) with MHS Inc. and is considered to be an international expert on the integration of emotional intelligence and leadership development.

In addition to his consulting practice, David teaches at two local universities and one foreign university (University of the West Indies, Trinidad) and provides services to the Canadian Centre for Management Development in Ottawa. David is also active on the executive of the International Society for Performance Improvement as Past President of the Vancouver Chapter.

CHRISTOPHER MILLS is Managing Director of Core Measures, a consulting company specializing in measuring and managing performance with offices in Singapore and Shanghai. A British-born Singapore PR who has worked and lived in Asia for over 20 years, he has worked with over 100 organizations in 14 countries and audited, designed, and facilitated over 70 strategy and performance management related projects.

He received his first Masters degree from the University of Wales. He also holds an MA in Human Resources from George Washington University. He has an Advanced Postgraduate Diploma in Management Consultancy from Henley Management College in the United Kingdom. He also studied at the Universities of Leeds and Southampton where he specialized in

English and Psychology. His Doctorate in Business Administration research focused on Performance Management. He was also a full-time lecturer at the National University of Singapore throughout the 1980s.

He has authored three books on performance management and over a dozen articles, the latest book titled *Performance Management Under The Microscope: A study of performance management practices in Singapore* published by the Singapore Human Resource Institute.

DATUK K.Y. MUSTAPHA has been State Secretary of Sabah, Malaysia, since April 2000. He completed a Bachelor of Arts degree in Anthropology and Sociology at the University of Malaya. He career has been within the Chief Minister's Department of Sabah. Prior to his present post, he was Permanent Secretary of Ministry of Communications and Works. He has facilitated workshops on government and public service issues such as "Reinventing Government Facilitators" and also spoke at the 1999 MS ISO Management Representative Workshop on "Professionalism of the Public Service – An Expectation For The New Millennium".

PUTRI JULIANI JOHARI is the Learning Research and Development Manager at Petronas Management Training Centre, PERMATA. With 20 years' experience mostly in the area of human resources development and human resources management, she has been actively involved in several corporate HR improvement and learning management initiatives in her organization. Within Petronas, she has worked with Insurance and Property Management, Training and Staff Development, Planning and Development, Salary Administration and Compensation, Personnel Policies and Evaluation, Management Training, Staff Development, Corporate Leadership Development, Learning Intervention and Learning Assessment and PMNTSB. She holds a Masters degree in Public Administration (MPA) from University of Southern California and a Bachelor of Arts (English) (Hons) from the University of Malaya.

NA BOON CHONG is the head of Hewitt Associates in Singapore. His expertise lies in organization strategy and diagnosis, and the alignment of people processes. He consults in diverse areas such as executive and professional compensation, performance measurement and management, competency development and organization design. Previously, his responsibility was in the practice and market development for ORC, Inc. He was also with Hay as a senior consultant in integrated compensation and human resource consulting. He consults with major organizations in the public sector. Boon graduated from the University of Minnesota and Rutgers University with a B.Sc. and M.Sc. respectively. He is accredited by the American Compensation Association as a Certified Compensation Professional.

AYMAN ADHAIR is Managing Director of the International Public Services Practice of BearingPoint, and has been actively involved in developing many strategic e-Government initiatives and promoting electronic delivery of government services by utilization of IT in the provision of Local and Federal Government services. Those of his initiatives that have been utilized include the Abu Dhabi Crown Prince Court initiative for the establishment of a Government Centre for Policy, Performance and Innovation based on a common government-wide information infrastructure; Sharjah Government for Cross Government Computerisation; and more recently, the development of vision and strategy for the State of Qatar Electronic Government Initiative. He is also responsible for developing the business case for starting the Government of Montenegro e-Government Initiative. He was recently elected a member of the United Nation Information and Communication Technology Task Force Bureau for the Arab Countries to support sustainable socio-economic development.

GARY YOUNG is Head of Learning and Development in Brunei Shell Petroleum Company (BSP), and manages the Learning and Development Centre in Seria. In 1976, he graduated with honours in Mechanical Engineering from Leeds University, England. He then joined Brunei LNG as mechanical engineer. After five years, he made a career change to HR. In HR, he has served in several capacities — as personnel planning and resourcing adviser, as housing and amenities officer, as head of technical and management training, as organizational effectiveness consultant, and currently as head of L&D. He has worked for Shell in Nigeria, Australia and Holland during his 28-year career. His key interests in BSP are leadership development and cultural change. In particular, he is very keen on the development of graduates. Recently, he revised and implemented a mentoring scheme and is piloting a shadow-coaching programme for selected graduates in BSP.

GERARDO PLANA is Executive Director of the Personnel Management Association of the Philippines (PMAP). He has worked as Executive Trainer since 1978 and delivered training programmes to more than 100 companies in the Philippines. He is also a Certified Professional in the

International Public Management Association and a Secretary General in Asia Pacific Federation of Human Resource Management (APFIIRM). Since 1990, he has been a faculty member of the Human Resource Management Development Center (HRMDC) at PMAP. He was speaker in the National HR Conference of Colombo, Sri Lanka, at a series of seminars on "Consulting Skills" in Malaysia, Bangladesh and Sri Lanka and at a seminar on "Personal Growth" in Indonesia.

ZAINAL ABIDDIN TINGGAL is Special Duties Officer at the Prime Minister's Office. His portfolio includes the civil service, the media and social affairs. Prior to this assignment, he was Deputy Director of the Civil Service Institute, an organization responsible for implementing HRD programmes for the civil service. Hs area of expertise is Human Resource Management and Development, Management, Public Policy and Communications. He started his career at Radio Television Brunei as a journalist during which time he was also a consultant for regional training programmes in journalism and media management. He has represented several organizations in regional and international meetings and delivered papers discussing Public Management and Human Resource Development. He completed his tertiary education both in Brunei and Singapore and attained his Masters in Communications in the United Kingdom.

LAURENCE SMITH is Vice President of Accenture Learning in Asia-Pacific. Previously, he worked at the World Bank as a Knowledge and Learning Adviser and for the Organizational Design Practice of McKinsey. He holds a Masters degree in Organizational Learning from the United States and a Bachelor in Organizational Studies from the United Kingdom. His area of work and study for the last 19 years has been the impact of emerging technologies on emerging markets in the Asia Pacific. He is interested in exploring the ways countries and companies can jump the curve of competition and development by the intelligent use of knowledge, learning and technology.

PROF DR CHARTCHAI NA CHIANGMAI is Professor of Political Science at the National Institute of Development Administration, Thailand. He earned his Ph.D in Political Science from the University of Wisconsin-Madison, USA. He was awarded a Distinguished Research Award in 1990 by the National Research Council of Thailand. He was Director of the National Institute of Development Administration at the Training Centre from 1988 to 1990. He is a member of the Asian Regional

Training and Development Organization, Social Science Association of Thailand and Political Science Association of Thailand. He is the author of *Administrative Manual of Service Delivery in Rural Development*, *Meeting New Demands*, *Civil Society in Thailand*, *"Duj Fon Sahalom Din Thi Haeng Paak" Development Paradigm of "King Rama 9th's NEW THEORY"* and *Holistic Development Management*.

KAREN ONG is Managing Director of Specialist Management Resources. She is a learner-oriented trainer with over twenty years of experience. Her experience with a Fortune 100 automobile company and Malaysia's leading television station has given her great reference in the relation of training to workplace environments. As well as being an SMR Accredited Training Professional (ATP), she also possesses a Certificate in Training and Development from CIPD, the United Kingdom. In addition, she is also a Zenger-Miller certified trainer (Frontline Leadership). Her training style is participative and friendly, and has benefited participants from Malaysia, Singapore, India, Taiwan, Japan and USA.

VICTOR S.L. TAN is Managing Director of KL Strategic Change Consulting Group. He has more than 25 years of experience in consulting, banking, strategic planning and training. He holds a Bachelor of Science from Elmira College, New York and an MBA from the Ohio State University, Columbus, Ohio, USA. He has won the Phi Beta Kappa Award, the highest academic honour given for overall achievement for American universities. To date, he has trained over 350,000 individuals in the area on managing change. His clients include American Express, Bank Negara Malaysia, BMG Malaysia, BMG Entertainment International, Chief Minister's Department, Sarawak, Dell Asia, Felda Plantations, Fujitsu Microelectronics (M), MIMOS. He has won several public speaking championships from the Institute of Bankers Malaysia and has had more than 300 of his management articles published in *The Banker's Journal*, *Malaysian Business*, *The New Straits Times*, *The STAR*, *The Executive Today*, the *Malaysian Tatler* and others.

PRAKASH ROHERA is Director of The RedwoodEdge, and has been involved in training for the last 11 years both in India and overseas. Prior to that, he worked with Citibank N.A. and the Bank of America N.T. & S.A. and has conducted more than 1,250 programmes so far in India and other countries. His eleven-year experience in leading organizations ranges from front-line sales & customer service functions to branch management and from sales management to human resources. Previously, he was Head of Customer Services & Operations with Bank of America, New Delhi. He set up a training firm "The Corporate Trainers" in 1991.

ANTHONY O'HARA has nine years of experience working with the leading e-Business technology and solutions vendor, Oracle Corporation. He has first-hand experience of the business transformation being driven by information technology and the Internet. In addition, his senior role within Oracle Corporation Asia Pacific has afforded him the privilege of working with government organizations and companies in a diverse range of industries and countries, and learning their business issues and priorities first-hand. His broad experience gained over 18 years in the IT industry has encompassed many roles and business settings. Anthony has worked on many government projects including in the areas of HRMS, Payroll, Financial Management, and Materials Management, amongst others.